MENTORING MATTERS

TARGETS, TECHNIQUES, AND TOOLS FOR BECOMING A GREAT MENTOR

Foreword by *New York Times* bestselling author

ORRIN WOODWARD

MENTORING MATTERS

First Edition, August 2013
10 9 8 7 6 5 4

Published by:

 Obstaclés Press
200 Commonwealth Court
Cary, NC 27511

Visit us at:
lifeleadership.com

ISBN 978-0-9895763-1-4

Design and Layout by Norm Williams, nwa-inc.com

Printed in the United States of America

The LIFE Leadership Essentials Series

Financial Fitness
Mentoring Matters

Excellent mentoring is the natural
result of learning the important
lessons of life and then caring enough
to help others learn them as well.

CONTENTS

FOREWORD

Great leaders are first great students. Indeed, if a person is too "big" to follow, then he or she is too small to lead. Good mentoring wisdom lives on in the students long after the mentor is gone. For instance, Socrates mentored Plato, who then mentored Aristotle, who then mentored Alexander the Great! Clearly, the wisdom, belief, and encouragement from a mentor to a mentee can literally change world history.

> **Good mentoring wisdom lives on in the students long after the mentor is gone.**

A good mentor is someone who has successfully journeyed down a trail similar to that of his mentee. In fact, it is the mentor's experience and wisdom from his journey that makes his time so valuable to the student. Newton once said, "If I have seen further, it is by standing on the shoulders of giants."

In essence, everyone, in his or her field, stands upon the shoulders of giants because there is no such thing as an entirely self-made person. The only real question is whose shoulders will a person stand upon? In other words, what results do they have in the learner's area of interest? Best-selling author Tim Marks elaborated on this thought, stating, "Define what you want, learn from someone who has gone before you, and then do it for the glory of God."

However, once a person finds a mentor, he must prove himself worthy of the mentor's investment. In my opinion, the best leadership line from any movie is when William Wallace spoke to his cavalry leader, saying, "Do it, and let them see you do it."

Likewise, mentees should listen, learn, and apply any advice offered by proven mentors. Mentoring isn't psychological analysis, where people talk for hours about their past. Rather, it's a plan of action in the present to change one's future.

A good mentor helps develop a plan for the mentee to implement. Then, when the mentee has completed the task or at least done everything humanly possible while failing on the battlefield, they gather again to PDCA[1]—Plan, Do, Check, Adjust—the good, the bad, and the ugly.

Interestingly, without the mentee's application, the mentoring process is practically worthless. The sobering statement, "When all is said and done, much more is said than is ever done," drives the mentee to apply the mentor's advice before meeting again.

Personally, I imagine how much it would cost to buy a top leader's time and then ensure that my efforts go above and beyond his expectations to validate the investment of his nonrenewable resource—his time. Mentees must apply what they have learned, and in the process, they will gain more time from mentors and learn even more so they can *do* even more.

The best mentors refuse to give away this precious resource of time; therefore, before agreeing to mentor, they ensure the student is hungry and driven. Probably the best way to explain this is through sharing a personal experience.

When I was a young man, my siblings and I would spend a month each year at my grandfather's farm in northern Michigan. One of the tasks my grandpa taught me was how to milk a cow. Although I was not particularly excited about this assignment, I did what I was told. After filling up a bucket of milk and setting it to the side, I noticed that the cream consistently coagulated on the surface. In fact, I noticed the same phenomenon repeated every day after I milked the cow.

Similarly, leaders, like cream, rise in any organization. A mentor's role is to ensure he has enough buckets of milk so he can choose from many worthy cream candidates for mentoring. In truth, I am not nearly as good a mentor as my good students make me look; conversely, I am not nearly as bad a mentor as my bad students make me appear.

It is the student's hunger and drive that makes all the difference, mainly because, since the mentor has already applied in his own life the advice he is giving the mentee, it is now up to the mentee to apply it to gain the same results. The only remaining question is: *Will* the mentee apply the advice he has been given?

Personally, I have been blessed with wonderful students because I learned to stop listening so much to what people say and start watching what they do. Just as cream rises to the top, hungry students will reveal themselves.

It is the mentor's role to play talent scout and identify the hungry students—not by their words but by their actions.

Success requires both opportunity and preparedness. In the case of mentoring, the mentor offers an opportunity to the prepared mentee; and if the student will implement it, success will happen.

The mentoring process matters because the success or failure of the next generation depends upon the quality of mentoring received. Furthermore, one's personal success depends in large part on his or her ability to effectively apply the advice from great mentors.

Accordingly, this book is filled with insights, nuggets, and techniques to help both mentors and mentees. Whether a person is an established leader looking to expand his or her ability to mentor or a hungry student looking to get on a mentor's radar screen, this book will help immensely.

Contained herein are seventy-seven specific tools to enhance the mentoring process. I cannot recommend this book highly enough and wish I might have had access to this information when I began my leadership journey. It has taken me decades to unpack the wisdom served up in this book.

> "Do it, and let them see you do it!"
> —William Wallace
> (Braveheart)

Author and business leader Jim Rohn (who mentored Tony Robbins, Mark Victor Hansen, Jack Canfield, and Brian Tracy, to name a few) said, "Success is neither

magical nor mysterious. Success is the natural consequence of consistently applying the basic fundamentals."

You hold in your hands a guide containing seventy-
seven fundamental tools to improve as a mentee and
mentor. Read it, ponder its lessons, and then implement
its teaching. Or, as William Wallace would say, "Do it, and
let them see you do it!"

—Orrin Woodward, two-time *New York Times* bestselling
author and co-founder of LIFE

PROLOGUE

Why Mentoring Is an Essential Skill
for Effective Leaders

Great leaders have great mentors. And most great leaders *are* great mentors. As Orrin Woodward wrote in the Foreword, Socrates mentored Plato, and Plato mentored Aristotle. Then Aristotle mentored Alexander the Great. In fact, find anyone in history whose name has "the Great" attached to it, and you'll find the person had a great mentor.

Warren Buffett mentored Bill Gates. Thomas Edison mentored Henry Ford. Steve Jobs was mentored by Robert Friedland, and Mark Zuckerberg considered Steve Jobs one of his mentors.

Almost the entire modern self-help industry was mentored, either directly or indirectly, by Buckminster Fuller—from Zig Ziglar and Napoleon Hill to Stephen Covey, Robert Kiyosaki, Ken Blanchard, and many others. One of the differences between good and great, as taught by Jim Collins, is excellent mentoring.

Two fantastic old movies that can really help us understand the importance of this skill are *Dead Poets Society* and *Ferris Bueller's Day Off.* If you haven't seen both of these classics, it's time to get some popcorn and have a movie night. In *Dead Poets Society*, the character played by Robin Williams is a great mentor. As a teacher, he comes into a traditional classroom and turns ordinary schooling into a truly great experience in learning, leadership, and life.

In comparison, the teacher in *Ferris Bueller's Day Off*, who famously repeats "Bueller, Bueller, Bueller..." in a monotone voice, is the prototypical example of how *not* to be a good mentor.

Great mentors are vital in education, business, career, and family. And learning from those who have gone before is what mentoring is all about. Without the benefit of mentors and their wisdom, each of us would have to blaze all new trails on our own, blindly learning through trial and error.

> **Great mentors are vital in education, business, career, and family. And learning from those who have gone before is what mentoring is all about.**

Indeed, it is the ability of mentors from one generation to pass on their knowledge and wisdom to rising generations that allows for all human progress.

The whole library of knowledge in all books on success and leadership makes up our shared human mentoring wisdom, what Stephen Covey called the "Wisdom Literature." The same is true in all great libraries, from the great books on leadership to the leading works on relationships and family success. In short, a great book is a collection of mentoring wisdom, and a great library is a compilation of many such books.

Leadership is essential to success on any level— personal, family, business, societal, and global—and mentoring is a vital facet of effective leadership. Find a great leader in history, and you'll find a quality mentor in his or her life. For every George Washington, you'll find a Colonel Fairfax; for every Abraham Lincoln, you'll find a Sarah Bush Johnston. Not all mentors are well known in history, but all great people owe a significant part of their success to the help and inspiration of their mentors.

People know what great mentoring is when they experience it. But explaining it sometimes feels like trying to tell someone what salt tastes like. When we experience it, we know it. But it is not easily defined or explained to people who haven't experienced it.

Somewhere along the line, fortunately, all of us have experienced great mentoring, a time when we fell deeply in love with learning,[2] made the choice to push outside our level of comfort, saw a whole new vision of what our life could be, or felt deeply inspired to do great things. Whatever caused these feelings mentored us because it touched us at a rarely reached level and deeply moved us.

Think of a time when you had such an experience. It may have been a person who inspired you, a movie you watched, music you heard, a story you read, or something else. Mentors come in many forms, but that feeling, that experience of wanting to change, to be better, is what great mentoring is all about.

Great mentors know how to create such feelings regularly, as often as they are needed. They know how to set the environment where such feelings and experiences are frequent, how to use such experiences to help us discover and improve ourselves, and even how to repeat such feelings so that our motivation and efforts are sustained. Great mentors care, and they are effective.

But being such a mentor isn't automatic. Each of us needs to learn from the best examples of great mentoring, to know the principles of effective mentoring, and to improve our ability to mentor those close to us. All of us need to learn how to successfully mentor more and better leaders.

Everyone has encountered good mentors and poor mentors, both in school and in our business lives. Think of the best business leader you ever had. What made him or her great as a leader? Did he care? Did she set a profound example? Did he share personal stories and work hard to keep you feeling inspired and motivated?

In contrast, think of the worst boss or manager you ever had. In what ways did she fail to inspire you and set a great example? Was he moody, temperamental, bossy, tyrannical, neglectful? Did she seem not to care about you personally or about helping you really succeed in life? Why was this person the "worst" leader you have encountered?

It has been said that in leadership, example isn't the most important thing — it's the only thing. And most excellence in leadership is connected with effective mentoring. Who are the most important mentors in your life? For example, who was your most important family mentor? Who was your top mentor in your youth and educational experiences? A coach? A teacher? A scouting, community, or church leader? Perhaps the author of a book that really helped you? Who has provided the most important mentoring in your career and work life? Who do you think of when you hear the words *"Great Mentor"*? Take a moment to mentally list them.

This quick stroll down memory lane can motivate you to become the leader you want to be. Remembering what made your own mentors great, as well as where they struggled, and striving to emulate their best qualities can make a big difference in your own ability to effectively mentor the people you serve.

What kind of mentor are you? Are you more like the great mentors you thought of above or like some of those who weren't very good mentors? How can you improve? What kind of mentor do you want to be?

This all matters because the future of the world depends on quality mentoring. And the level of your personal success depends in large part on your ability to effectively follow great mentors and also to mentor others. In short, consider the following:

- The world never rises above the quality of its leaders; leadership determines destiny.
- The quality of our leaders is directly impacted by their ability to mentor others.
- A leader's ability to mentor others is determined by his or her mentoring skills, and such skills can be developed and improved.
- As we improve our mentoring skills and more effectively mentor others, we directly increase the quality of leadership in our world.

The path toward success is challenging, and those who try to follow it without the help of effective mentors seldom make it very far. Nearly all great achievements are the result of both effective mentoring and the corresponding humility to follow great mentors.

Great leaders, and those who are seeking to become great leaders, are constantly improving their mentoring abilities. This focus helps them identify great mentors who will help them continue to grow and progress, and it also directly upgrades the quality of their leadership skills.

Harvard researcher Howard Gardner wrote in Leading Minds that some leaders go through their lives always expecting to become great leaders, while others develop their leadership skills naturally over time as they progress in their personal and career experiences. But, interestingly, most leaders rise to leadership quite by surprise when some event or development in their life requires it of them. Gardner also suggests that there are four major kinds of leaders:

> **Great leaders, and those who are seeking to become great leaders, are constantly improving their mentoring abilities.**

- Direct leaders, who lead inspiringly from some official position of authority (Winston Churchill, Ronald Reagan).

- Innovative leaders, who lead by their surprising non-official influence on society (Einstein, Picasso, Sam Walton, Steve Jobs).
- Visionary leaders, who see a greater potential for humanity and help move society significantly in the direction of a more ideal world (Joan of Arc, Jefferson, Gandhi, Martin Luther King Jr., Jean Monnet [the founder of European Unity]).
- Ordinary leaders, who have the position or potential of great leadership but go through the motions rather than significantly changing the direction of their society, business, or arena of leadership. Gardner puts US President Gerald Ford and General Motors CEO Roger Smith in this category.

The fundamental difference between direct, innovative, and visionary leaders on the one hand and the less inspiring ordinary leaders on the other is that ordinary leaders typically fail to effectively mentor. Without quality mentoring of those they lead,

> **Masters are successful because they have mastered the basics.**

their leadership impact is limited, and their ability to lead is weakened. Even the best followers seldom get inspired by following leaders who fail to effectively mentor.

Again, think of the monotone droning of the teacher in Ferris Bueller's Day Off or of the worst teacher or manager you've ever had. Bad mentoring isn't really mentoring at all, just as bad leadership is actually a lack of leadership.

Basketball great Larry Bird put it this way: "First master the fundamentals." Masters are successful because they have mastered the basics, and these seventy-seven techniques are among the most basic fundamentals of mentoring.

So much depends on great mentoring. Our world doesn't need more ordinary leaders, but we certainly need more innovative, visionary, and great leaders—and we need them to be effective and inspiring mentors.

More to the point, the world needs you to be a great leader and an effective mentor, and the key to great mentoring is to master the basics.

1

THE FIRST LESSON OF MENTORING

The seventy-seven techniques of great mentoring outlined in this book are the basic fundamentals of great mentoring, and technique number one is the most basic of all. This first lesson of mentoring is simple: Allegiance to God and good comes first.

The *Oxford English Dictionary* defines *allegiance* as "loyalty or commitment to a superior person or to a group or cause." In history, a superior person was often royal or aristocratic, and the commoners' connection with a certain elite family or official was summarized in the way the elites were addressed: "My liege," "My liege lord," or "My lord."

Synonyms of *allegiance* include *loyalty, fidelity, faithfulness, obedience, homage*, and *devotion*. Many Americans know this word from the Pledge of Allegiance to the US flag. When we give allegiance to something, we love it, honor it, and put it above other things.

In our day, loyalty to aristocrats is little more than a relic of history, but our allegiances still determine much about us. Every time we make a choice, we do so with our top allegiance in mind—either consciously or subconsciously.

25

Our top allegiance is part of our full-time mental makeup and underpins every decision, whether we think about it or not.

Of course, everyone has more than one allegiance. We have allegiances and loyalties to our spouse, children, parents, friends, and perhaps a church, company, alma mater, political party, and other entities, including sports teams—often all at the same time.

Ultimately, however, each of us has one highest allegiance, a top priority that we are loyal to above all else. Some people hold this top allegiance to themselves, while many spend most of their lives trying above everything to impress others—from a certain person, such as a father- or mother-in-law, to groups of people, such as colleagues or fellow church members.

To be a good mentor, we must put our highest allegiance in the right place, which means to put God—or, if you prefer, good—above everything else.

An allegiance to God and good is vital to being a great mentor. This loyalty puts everything in your life in perspective and keeps you grounded through every challenge and struggle.

Choosing good as a higher allegiance than other people, loved ones, yourself, your reputation, your income, and everything else is one of the most important choices a leader can make. Putting God and good above everything else makes you capable of real leadership because it aligns you with the good things of the world rather than the selfish and self-centered focus of the ego or the wishy-washy and constantly shifting emphasis of trying to impress others.

This is the first lesson of great mentoring. Know who you are. Stand for something. Stand for the right and the good. And don't be moved from this allegiance to God and good, regardless of your circumstances. Great mentors must be solidly grounded.

2

VISION

Vision is required for success. Your vision of life, of your dreams and goals, and of who you want to become are essential to leadership and mentoring. Leaders with vision are able to inspire others to do the hard work and make the important choices that bring success. Lack of vision causes a lack of motivation, focus, and execution.

Orrin Woodward said, "Vision is tomorrow's reality expressed as an idea today." Seneca said, "To the person who does not know where he wants to go, there is no favorable wind." And James Allen famously wrote, "Dream lofty dreams, and as you dream, so shall you become. Your Vision is the promise of what you shall one day be. Your ideal is the prophecy of what you shall at last unveil."

An anonymous great thinker said, "Dissatisfaction and discouragement are not caused by the absence of things but the absence of vision." Nowhere is this more important than in mentoring. Each person you mentor will have his or her own vision and goals, and a key part of mentoring is helping the mentee or protégé answer these questions: "What is my vision? What are my greatest goals?"

There are two sides to mentoring vision. The first usually occurs early in your relationship with a mentee and consists of asking the person two crucial questions: (1) "What is your highest allegiance?" and (2) "What is your vision of your life's success?"

Talking with each mentee about his thoughts on these two questions is central to mentoring. By knowing where he puts his highest allegiance and where he wants to end up in life, you are "beginning with the end in mind," as Stephen Covey puts it, and can effectively help the mentee on his path to success.

If you have concerns or even disagreements with the mentee's allegiance or vision, it is best to know this and discuss them right from the beginning. When you catch on to a mentee's vision and want to support him in achieving it, you naturally become a more effective mentor.

> **Mentors help their mentees turn vision into visualizing.**

The second side of mentoring vision is helping your mentee keep it in mind as he progresses through the many struggles, the ups and downs, of achieving his goals and dreams. For example, Kenneth Labich wrote, "Don't underestimate the power of a vision. McDonald's founder,

Ray Kroc, pictured his empire long before it existed, and he saw how to get there."

Mentors help their mentees turn vision into visualizing. Most of those who eventually obtain success have learned to envision their goals becoming reality—many times, consistently over the years. Vision is vital, and it must be turned into the daily habits of visualizing and envisioning.

The poet Jonathan Swift was correct: "Vision is the art of seeing the invisible." Former Notre Dame president Theodore Hesburgh said, "The very essence of leadership is [that] you have a vision. It's got to be a vision you articulate clearly and forcefully on every occasion. You can't blow an uncertain trumpet."

Ronald Reagan affirmed this principle: "To grasp and hold a vision, that is the very essence of successful leadership...." And Mark Twain summed it up with his characteristically insightful wisdom: "You cannot depend on your eyes when your imagination is out of focus."

WORKSHOP

1. Take a few minutes to write out your life purpose, a vision of your ideal life. Just brainstorm and write what you really want to be, do, and become and how you want to serve. Also, how do you want the world to be different because of your life?

   This exercise is well worth your time. If you've never done it before, it may take longer than a few minutes. You may need to set aside a certain amount of time over the course of several days, but don't give up. Put your heart into this, and articulate your goals and how they fit into your life mission.

Note, of course, that your life probably won't directly follow everything you write. But the very act of thinking through your best life and putting it into writing will have a positive influence on your life and leadership.

2. Once you have written your life vision, read it every day for a month. Make edits or changes when they occur to you. After the first month, continue to read your vision frequently.

3. Now, help each person you mentor do steps 1 and 2 above. This will help them focus their resources on what's really important on their path to success.

4. When and if it feels appropriate, discuss your life vision with those you mentor and invite them to share their purpose with you. Knowing the goals of your mentor and mentees can significantly improve the quality of progress toward realizing your goals and living your mission.

3

THE FIVE LEVELS OF INFLUENCE

In their book *Launching a Leadership Revolution*, authors Chris Brady and Orrin Woodward wrote about the five levels of influence, teaching that understanding each is an important skill for great leaders. These levels include:

1. Learning
2. Performing
3. Leading
4. Developing leaders
5. Developing leaders who develop leaders

Great mentoring is all about levels four and five. Chris and Orrin said, "When we wrote the book, we didn't know it would become a *New York Times*, *Wall Street Journal*, and *USA Today* bestseller. We didn't know that many thousands of people would embrace it and use it to build companies that build leaders. But we did know that leadership is only level 3, and that even more important than leadership is developing leaders."

In short, the greatest mentors don't mentor only those they work with directly. Rather, they think of the people their mentees will mentor and even those who will be mentored four or five generations ahead, and they help their mentees become the type of mentors who can become great mentors of mentors.

> **"Even more important than leadership is developing leaders."**
> **—Chris Brady and Orrin Woodward**

For example, consider how this works in a family setting. Some people focus on their career as the center point of life. Ask most people what they do in life, and they'll say they're a doctor, attorney, accountant, business-person, engineer, or some other profession.

Sometimes, in contrast, we meet people who answer the same question by saying, "I'm a dad," "I'm a father to three great children," or "I'm a wife and mother." While this cheeky answer frequently indicates that the person has given a lot of thought to his or her life purpose and priorities, the truth is that there is an even better way.

On one level, we can focus on our work life as the center of our purpose.

At a higher level, we can make our marriage and parental relationships the top priority.

At an even better level, we can be the kind of parents who wisely and consciously raise our grandkids—even when our own kids are just little. This means thinking through what we're really doing as parents. Are we just career people who happen to have kids? Hopefully not.

Likewise, are we spouses and parents raising kids to be confident, contributing adults? This is a good step.

Or are we, above all, future grandparents who are raising our kids to be fantastic parents who themselves will raise their children in a way that positively influences several generations to come? Those who see their role in such far-reaching generational terms will approach their marriage and parenting in a purposeful way.

The same applies to business mentoring. If we mentor only the people with whom we work directly, we won't be as helpful to them as if we see our role as one of mentoring them to be great mentors of mentors.

WORKSHOP

Make a list of the individuals you currently mentor. Get a notebook and write the name of each person at the top of a fresh page. Now, go to the first page, read the name at the top, and ask yourself, "How can I help this person not only achieve his or her goals but become a great mentor of mentors who will help many people for generations to come?"

This is a big question, but it helps you be a great mentor to consider the lasting potential of the person you mentor. The person may seem incapable or weak now, but what is her potential? Who might she become? How can you help?

> **Mentoring is so powerful precisely because the mentor often sees the forest, while the mentee is focused on the trees.**

What would she have to do to become a great oak rather than a small acorn?

Most importantly, what is the first thing she would need to do? What is the first thing you can do to help her get started?

Mentoring is so powerful precisely because the mentor often sees the forest, while the mentee is focused on the trees. But this only occurs when mentors take the time to brainstorm the potential of their mentees, to think about what they need, and to help them get started.

Once you have done this with one mentee in mind, do it for another. Repeat this exercise with each person you mentor, and write your thoughts on each individual's page.

Then, when you have finished this brainstorming session, meet with your mentees and help them take their next step. Start by asking them, not telling them. You already have a written list of what you think they need, but begin by asking them what they think they need to do to become great leaders and mentors of mentors. Then discuss their answers in ways that help them take specific, measurable action.

This is the actual work of mentoring—brainstorming on your own and then discussing and planning a course of action together.

4

UTILIZE GREAT BOOKS

The more that you read, the more things you will know. The more that you learn, the more places you'll go.

— DR. SEUSS

The greatest books of human history create a collection of ideas by great mentors. They span both fiction and nonfiction and include mentors in all fields, from leadership and family to art and science, from technology and entertainment to media and education, from engineering and happiness to sales and medicine, from law and accounting to marriage, cinema, music, architecture, software programming, modern trivia, management theory, nineteenth-century French poetry, and so forth.

In short, the classics are the library of great mentoring in every field, topic, and branch of human endeavor. And many modern classics are being written each decade, books that move people to action and change the world.

One important role for mentors is to help their protégés become widely read and thus become men and women of substance who are acquainted with great ideas in many fields. The best way to do this, of course, is by example. Then, along with a solid foundation of classics, the mentor will want to suggest important books and readings that deal with current mentee needs, challenges, and projects.

Leaders are readers, and great leaders are great readers.

To get a handle on the great ideas, here are a few valuable resources. The *Great Books* series by Britannica is a good place to start, as is the equally excellent collection titled the *Harvard Classics*. Or mentors can simply send mentees to the library to start reading important books they've heard about but never read, works by Plato or Shakespeare, for example.

The key is to read. Start reading great books, and keep reading. Great books are the mentors of great thinking, and no skill is more valuable to leadership than effective thinking. This is the learning method of Einstein and Churchill, Lincoln and Twain, Jefferson and Gandhi, Abigail Adams and Jane Austen, and many others.

Jefferson went so far as to say, "I cannot live without books." He also wrote, "Books

> **Great books are the mentors of great thinking.**

constitute capital....It is not, then, an article of mere consumption but fairly of capital, and often in the case of professional men, setting out in life, it is their only capital." Reading great works, ancient and modern, is an investment in yourself because it helps you become a person of substance who understands the great conversation of leading people through history.

Thoreau said, "Read the best books first, or you may not have a chance to read them all." Moreover, leaders share a great mastermind with others who've read the same books. Author Margaret Mahy wrote: "I think books create a sort of network in the reader's mind, with one book reinforcing another. Some books form relationships. Other books stand in opposition. No two writers or readers have the same pattern of interaction."

Thomas Carlyle said, "What we become depends on what we read after all the professors have finished with us. The greatest university of all is a collection of books." Mortimer Adler went deeper: "In the case of good books, the point is not to see how many of them you can get through, but how many can get through to you."

Ray Bradbury understood just how important the great books are to the future of prosperity and freedom: "You don't have to burn books to destroy a culture. You just get people to stop reading them." And Descartes may have summed it up best: "The reading of all good books is like a conversation with the finest minds of past centuries."

Again, leaders are readers, and great leaders are great readers. To restate the levels of influence, great leaders help others become great readers, and the best leaders help leaders become readers who help other leaders become readers.

Read more great books, and by doing so, you will expand the number of your great mentors by adding the greatest authors of history as your teachers.

5

WHERE TO START

So far, we've learned about four things to do when you first begin mentoring a new person. First, help him clarify his allegiance; second, help him identify his vision for his career and life. Once these two internal decisions are made and verbalized, help your mentee learn the five levels of influence and begin to see himself not just as a potential leader but as a budding builder of leaders and later a leader of leaders of leaders. Fourth, teach him the importance of great reading, and help him begin reading important books and the truly great ideas of Scripture and humankind. Help your protégé become a person of substance who is part of the great conversation among leaders through history.

> **In short, learn about personality types, and you learn more about each person you mentor.**

With these four principles applied, you can begin to emphasize several more mentoring lessons. The first four were all questions you got the mentee asking about himself. In contrast, the next three items are more about questions to ask yourself about your new mentee.

Chris Brady and Orrin Woodward wrote the following:

There are three main areas to identify when beginning to mentor someone. First is his or her personality or natural temperament. Since the ancient philosophers, there has been an awareness that each of us arrives at birth with a basic personality temperament. It is beyond the scope of this book to delve into this in any detail, but leaders must know which of the temperaments are dominant in their protégés. Second, there are different learning styles. Some people learn best through visual instruction, others learn verbally, and still others learn best experientially.

Third is the concept of "love languages." These are the styles of communication that a person prefers, such as verbal, touch, receiving gifts, quality time, and acts of service.

Knowing these natural bents allows a mentor to provide spot-on instruction specifically tailored to the maximum impact on the individual being developed. This is not as complicated as it might first appear. Light reading on the topics of learning styles, love languages, and temperaments can familiarize you enough to understand and be able to identify how a given protégé is naturally inclined. This will facilitate the leadership-development process in tremendous ways.[3]

In short, learn about personality types, and you learn more about each person you mentor by identifying her personality type(s), learning style(s), and love language(s).

WORKSHOP

Pull out your notebook that has the names of the people you mentor at the top of various pages. Go to a page with one of your mentees listed at the top, and identify his personality type. (If you need to, find a resource on personality types and study it. We recommend *Personality Plus* by Florence Littauer.)

Note several things about the person's personality type that will help you mentor him or her. If you don't know your mentee well enough to do this, it may not be time to make her a protégé just yet. Or, if it is, then get to know her well enough to identify her personality type.

Now consider your mentee's learning style and love language, and write it on the page. Brainstorm ways this will help you mentor him. If you haven't read *The 5 Love Languages* by Gary Chapman, now is a good time.

As for learning style, simply ask yourself, "Does she learn best by seeing? By listening? By talking? By experiencing? In a particular combination of those styles? Or in some other way?" For example, some people learn best by arguing, others by going to nature and pondering. Think about your mentee, and then write your thoughts on the mentee's page in your notebook.

Once you have listed a personality style, learning style, and love language for your mentee, make a few notes on how this information can help you be a better mentor to him or her.

Repeat this process for each person you mentor.

6

ASK YOURSELF QUESTIONS

In addition to identifying temperament, love languages, and personality types, mentors can learn a lot about their mentees simply by taking the time to ask some important questions.

In the book *The Student Whisperer*, the authors listed the following important questions mentors should ask themselves about their mentees:

- What kind of mentor am I for this mentee right now?
- What walls or roadblocks is my mentee facing?
- What is the next step for my mentee?
- What is my mentee's "Inner Critic" telling my mentee?
- Does my mentee seem to be listening to some other negative voice, and if so what is that voice telling her?
- What kind of mentor does my mentee need me to be right now?
- What changes do I need to make to effectively be the mentor my mentee needs right now?[4]

41

The answers to such questions are extremely helpful to you as a mentor. In fact, the very process of asking and thinking about such questions makes you a better, more effective mentor and leader.

> **The very process of asking and thinking about such questions makes you a better, more effective mentor and leader.**

In short, begin mentoring by getting your mentee to ask some important questions about herself, and follow up by spending the time to ask yourself important questions that help you get to know your mentee better.

Chris Brady and Orrin Woodward listed the additional following questions to ask about your mentee:

- What makes him tick?
- What makes him special?
- Why did he get involved in his particular field?
- What motivates him?
- What challenges has he had in his life?
- What victories has he had?
- What principles does he understand and embody?
- What principles does he still need to learn?
- What blind spots does he have about himself?
- What is his commitment level?
- What is the basis of his character?
- Where is his thinking?[5]

One of the most important roles of mentoring is asking questions. Great mentors ask these kinds of questions about their protégés, and they take action based on the answers. Mediocre and poor mentors try to get by without asking and responding to these questions.

WORKSHOP

Ask each of the questions in this chapter about each person you closely mentor. Write the answers in your notebook. Also, take at least one action for each protégé based on this exercise.

Return to this exercise periodically.

7
_____

THE PHASES OF LIFE

Personality types, temperament, love languages, and various other questions mentors ask about their mentees can greatly improve the quality of mentoring. Another valuable model that can be extremely useful for mentors is life stages.

All of us pass through various phases of life as we grow up and grow older. Knowing what stage your mentee is in can help you mentor her more effectively.

For example, developmental psychologist Erik Erickson taught that there are eight major stages of life, each based on natural psychological development:

1. From birth through age one, most people work out the major issues of trust versus mistrust, and the central theme of this stage is hope.

2. From ages one to three, children progress through the autonomy versus shame/doubt stage, and the main lesson of this phase is willpower.

3. From ages three to six, the focus is on initiative versus guilt, with a major theme of purpose.

4. From six to twelve, most kids struggle with industry versus inferiority, and the main lesson is competence.

Note that for mentors of children, especially parents and teachers,[6] understanding these first four developmental stages is extremely helpful.

5. From ages twelve to eighteen, the youth ages, the central challenge is identity versus role confusion, which is one of the reasons the teenage years can be difficult for both youth and their parents. The central question of this stage is fidelity, which usually translates for girls as "Am I worthy of love?" and to boys as "Will I ever measure up?"[7]

   Fathers and mothers can be extremely helpful in mentoring youth during this stage, especially if they understand the challenges.

Not surprisingly, mentoring adults presents different challenges than teaching youth, and for many people mentoring adults is a significant focus within our careers and leadership roles.

6. Between ages eighteen and forty, most people deal with the major issues of intimacy versus isolation, and the central theme is love.

7. From around ages forty to sixty-five, the focus is on generativity versus stagnation (another way to say this is vibrancy versus living in a rut). The major defining lesson is care.

8. Finally, after age sixty-five, the central struggle is often ego integration (legacy) versus despair, and the main theme is wisdom.

For mentors of adults, your protégé's stage has a significant impact on his life and therefore on how to most effectively mentor him.

Many mentors simultaneously work with protégés in several adult stages of progress. On any given day, you will likely mentor people from all four major personality types, several love languages, different learning styles, various different temperaments—not to mention a range of minor categories of personality types—and in all three adult life stages.

If you have or work with children, you might be mentoring people from all eight life stages and the many various other types all at the same time! In short, the reason mentoring works so much better than any "one size fits all" approach to leadership is that individuals are different.

By mentoring each individual in a personalized way, you help all those you lead to learn, progress, and succeed more effectively than by trying to fit them into one box.

Thinking, and especially leading, outside the box isn't just the new way; it's the only way.

Individualization and personalization are essential parts of leadership. Of course, some things like rules and policies need to be common for all, but mentoring must be unique, or it will lose its effectiveness.

> **By mentoring each individual in a personalized way, you help all those you lead to learn, progress, and succeed more effectively than by trying to fit them into one box.**

For mentees ages eighteen to forty, remember to emphasize their importance to you, to the team, and to each other. Help them learn to work together with their spouse, where applicable, and to keep work, no matter how important, in its proper place behind their marriage, kids, and family. Help them realize and frequently reiterate the importance of hard work, of doing the right things over and over, and of not giving up.

During this stage of life, focusing on balance in areas like health, finances, family, and work doesn't always come naturally, but it is very important to your protégés. Many struggles are solved by helping them put aside work for a few days to focus on strengthening a romantic relationship or spending quality time with a child or parent.

Remember that the key word in this stage is love. If your protégé is between eighteen and forty and struggling, some kind of love issue—its lack, excess, or imbalance—is often the culprit. This can mean the obvious relationships with her spouse, parents, siblings, or children, or it can mean a lack of love with her colleagues, her friends, or her work. If she doesn't love her work, your mentoring will be different than if she is fighting with her spouse, for example.

For protégés ages forty to sixty-five, the key word is care. What do they really care about? What have they stopped caring about? What do they need to care about more, or less? Do they feel like their lives are vibrant and exciting or stuck in a rut?

Many people naturally believe that life gets easier as you live longer, but sages have long taught that many things in life get more challenging and complex as we age. This lesson is certainly helpful in mentoring people in the forty-to-sixty-five life stage. These people are almost certainly protégés now, not beginning mentees, even if you have just begun working with them. They are older, in the prime of their lives, experienced, and prone to lead more than when they were younger.

Their potential is great, and your mentoring can help them achieve in amazing ways. On the flip side, their mistakes tend to be more costly, and their struggles are likely more painful. For example, the dreaded midlife crisis, if it comes at all, will almost surely occur during this stage. Divorce and conflict with siblings, older children, and former business partners are at their climax during these decades.

On the one hand, therefore, mentoring forty-to-sixty-five-year-old protégés can be difficult, but on the other hand, if they need your help, they'll likely need it a lot. A genuinely good, caring mentor can make all the difference during such challenges. The most important thing a mentor can do for this stage's protégés is to really care, and, next to caring, the most important work is to really listen.

Many people at this point in their lives aren't fully aware of how much untapped potential they have. They can improve the world in great ways, and, as a caring mentor, you can help them by pointing out the great things you think they can do. For example, there are at least eight important roles each person can fulfill during this era of life:[8]

1. Mentoring and building more protégés
2. Filling in any gaps in their education and deepening their areas of expertise
3. Getting more actively involved as citizens and impacting politics, society, and public policy and leadership
4. Adding value by effectively leading and spreading more business success

5. Analyzing current trends and warning younger generations of coming challenges

6. Writing, composing, developing, and adding to the knowledge of our arts, sciences, and other fields of wisdom

7. Using donations, service, philanthropy, and investment to spread happiness and success

8. Finding ways to serve and lead more widely to significantly improve the community, society, nation, and world

The key to this stage is to help your protégés see things they really care about and bring their talents, abilities, and efforts to bear in making a noticeable difference in these things. Building a business is often the most motivating project during this period, especially if it incorporates several or all of the eight roles listed above.

At some point, usually after age sixty-five, the body slows down, and people are less energetic about actively leading. The role of a great mentor at this period is to help the protégé get deeply excited about leaving an important legacy. The scope of her efforts may become more focused at this point, but a mentor can help her continue to influence through the key ideas of legacy and wisdom.

> **Protégés need mentors at every stage of life, and great mentors can help their mentees truly succeed through all the phases.**

Protégés need mentors at every stage of life, and great mentors can help their mentees truly succeed through all the phases. In summary, great mentors emphasize the following as they personalize their mentoring with each protégé:

Mentee Age	Mentor Emphasis with Protégé
18–40	Doing the hard work to build and grow something important and keeping priorities in their proper place
40–65	Staying vibrant and enthusiastic by taking on big projects that achieve important goals and fulfill one's life purpose
65+	Sharing wisdom and leaving a legacy

8

THE SIZE OF YOUR VISION

How many times have you heard an adult tell a child to "be realistic" or "get real" or heard a boss or manager tell an employee or colleague that his or her dreams are impossible, impractical, or too idealistic?

Sometimes it is appropriate to give this kind of advice, but too often we shut down somebody's dreams instead of helping the people we work with rise to the level of their aspirations. Thoreau said, "If you have built castles in the air, your work need not be lost; that is where they should be. Now put the foundations under them."

Well-meaning leaders sometimes err on the side of telling a protégé to "stop dreaming" and at other times by discounting one's dream as "thinking too small."

The key is for great mentors to embrace the mentee's dreams just as they are—and then optimistically talk about the big ways these dreams can make a difference and also about the small things the mentee will need to do to make the dreams a reality. Great mentors are skilled at reframing. Author Oliver DeMille wrote:

> The key is for great mentors to embrace the mentee's dreams just as they are—and then optimistically talk about the big ways these dreams can make a difference and also about the small things the mentee will need to do to make the dreams a reality.

My vision of my life is to help create and eventually see Good Government Worldwide! This means that every person in the world will someday live in a society where he or she enjoys true freedom—spiritual, political, and economic.

Imagine how many times I've been told that this dream is too big, too idealistic, impossible, and "never going to happen." But this is still my vision, and my life is still dedicated to making this happen.

Fortunately, in contrast to the many who have laughed in response to my dream or told me, "Get real, Oliver!," I had a fabulous mentor early on who took a different approach. When I told W. Cleon Skousen that my dream was Good Government Worldwide, and that I felt my mission in life was to help this become a reality, he looked me right in the eyes, nodded reassuringly, and asked seriously, "What is your first step?"

He took a "pie-in-the-sky" dream of an idealistic kid and reframed it immediately as a realistic question about something I could practically do right away. That's great mentoring.

My response? I just melted! I mean, my heart just opened up and I became incredibly humble to whatever suggestions he had. After so many people seeing my dream as crazy, outlandish, unattainable, silly or downright ridiculous, his genuinely respectful response and question was literally like the old cliché of giving water to someone dying of thirst.

When I told him my first step was to read all the books he had authored, he nodded thoughtfully, then replied, "Actually, you might want to start by reading the great classical and English thinkers. That's where the American founders started. I could suggest a few titles if you want." I immediately pulled out my pen and notebook, and I became a dedicated mentee.

The power of dreams is real, and the power of a mentor who respects dreams and helps the mentee reframe them for success is essential to leadership.

On another occasion, Dr. Skousen asked me how much money I planned to make from a business project I was engaging. I told him a modest amount, and instead of telling me to dream much bigger, he simply replied. "Excellent goal. Tell me, Oliver, what if you succeed well beyond your plans and you make ten or a hundred times that? What will you do with the extra money?"

> It's hard to overstate how important your mentee's dreams are. After all, they're *his* dreams!

I thoughtfully considered the question (who wouldn't?), and as I attempted to answer him my dreams suddenly—and permanently—expanded. His gentle reframing changed my vision.

My dream hasn't come yet, but it will—maybe in my lifetime, maybe after. But it will. And I'll keep spending my whole life working toward it regardless of what anyone thinks. Thank you, Cleon Skousen. The day of your funeral I stood in the parking lot, leaned on my car, and wept for over an hour. Great mentors are, well, great.

It's hard to overstate how important your mentee's dreams are. After all, they're *his* dreams! They may be too small in your estimation, or they may be too idealistic, unrealistic, or downright crazy. But effective mentors don't argue about a protégé's dreams. They do, however, ask wise questions that get the mentee thinking.

Many people have unrealistic dreams, and others have dreams that are too small for them, below their potential. But they still feel their dreams.

That's how dreams are. We can allow skepticism or struggle to crush them, but nobody else can do that without our consent. So when a mentor, or potential mentor, takes our dream seriously and asks us what the first step is, big dreams can become real. At the very least, they'll get started in the right direction.

Effective mentors learn how to reframe to help their mentees see things in bigger ways or in smaller steps as needed.

9

WHEN TO EMAIL, CALL, OR MEET

Effective mentoring is not just about what the mentor says, but also about the environment in which he speaks. One of the quickest ways to ruin your credibility with your mentees is to break the basic rules of when to e-mail, call, or meet. The rules of thumb are simple:

If anything negative or difficult is going to be discussed, don't e-mail or text.

If it is potentially *very* negative or difficult, meet.

If the potential positive impact of the thing to be discussed is huge, meet.

If your mentee is going to hear about a major negative or super positive on social media before you can meet, call right away. Then meet.

As for Skype or Google Hangout, take the time to think it through. If meeting in person would be significantly better, and if the meeting matters a lot, meet.

Not many meetings are better than no meetings, so keep meetings to a minimum. But when something is very important, nothing beats a face-to-face conversation.

An occasional call, e-mail, or text just because you care is very nice. You don't have to have an agenda; just say, "I was thinking about you and called to see how you're doing."

10

PAY ATTENTION TO NONVERBAL CUES

It has been said that we humans tend to communicate about 10 percent verbally and about 90 percent nonverbally. This is an important reality for mentors. We need to pay attention—especially to things nonverbal.

For example, Oliver DeMille and Tiffany Earl wrote:

> You know your mentee is learning if he is laughing, crying, sighing, grunting, or dancing. These are good signs. Sometimes we get discouraged when we see tears. Sometimes we hold back and don't laugh. Laughter can be great mentoring. Growls and grunts can be wonderful.
>
> Know and recognize the many ways a mentee can demonstrate that he is learning and that you are having influence. Brainstorm how you can improve on this with each mentee.[9]

Mentors must pay attention. This is a central part of good leadership.

11

THE SPIRIT OF "AND"

Former eBay COO Maynard Webb teaches that one key to leadership and mentoring is to help people get and keep the spirit of "and." This means that a good life is about more than just one purpose, as Webb puts it. He says we shouldn't look at career, family, and other facets of life as compartmentalized but rather holistically, though most people don't do this.[10]

This technique is very effective. Help your mentees dream big, list the goals they want to achieve in various parts of life, and consider how they can work toward all of them. Focus is important, even vital, to success, but so is the balance that comes by applying the spirit of "and."

Chris Brady wrote: "We have all heard that it is critical to 'major on majors,' that if we 'fit the big rocks in the jar we can always get the little ones in later,' and similar sayings. And these are all true. However, in our rush to simplify and focus, we must not forget that life is not that simple, and nobody accomplishes worthwhile goals without the ability to handle several things at once.

> "The key is to know which majors to major upon, and which minors not to disregard."
> —Chris Brady

"The key is to know which majors to major upon, and which minors not to disregard."[11] This doesn't mean giving in to the "distraction diseases" that most of us already suffer from; it means finding out which things really matter and giving them the time and energy they need, rather than letting them fall by the wayside.

Brady went on to explain that in knowing which details matter, as well as which can be disregarded, and then giving the details the attention they deserve, leaders are actually improving their ability to effectively focus.

Of course your mentee wants to be successful in business, and he will find more success by taking care of business *and* family *and* service *and* other important things rather than ignoring important things and only working on his career.

12

TACT

Orrin Woodward wrote that one of the "soft skills" of leadership from the Center for Creative Leadership's list is political savvy: the ability to influence people to obtain goals. He continued:

The heart of being politically savvy, according to CCL, is networking, reading situations, and thinking before speaking. This is an essential skill for mentors, and one that good mentors teach to their protégés.

Political savvy is the tact to say the truth that needs to be said, but in a way that doesn't damage the relationship more than the truth enhances the cause. Unfortunately, this may be one of the most violated of soft skills and why many potential leaders are without influence even though they have great ideas for improvement. Tact, therefore, is an essential quality to develop in working with others.

I define tact as the ability to influence others through using proper words and actions without offending the other party. Truth in love is the principle, but it is easier said than done.

For instance, how many meetings have the readers attended where truth needed to be told in order to move the meeting forward? However, instead of progressing in a tactful way towards this objective, someone, in contrast, went off on the other party, impaling him or her on the "sword of truth."

> "I define tact as the ability to influence others through using proper words and actions without offending the other party. Truth in love is the principle, but it is easier said than done."
> —Orrin Woodward

Predictably, the other party, instead of hearing the merits of the suggestion, responded to the attack personally and mounted an attack of his own on his antagonist. Both sides defend themselves and the meeting accomplishes nothing, but further damages relationships. In consequence, the truth exposed is buried under escalating emotions and the only real, but wrong, lesson learned is to not share truth at all. The team, in other words, has chosen peace rather than progress.

Thankfully, there is a better path. Indeed, a person who masters truth with tact is worth his weight in gold. Perhaps this leads the reader to the same series of questions I asked on my leadership journey. But, how is this essential leadership skill learned? Mainly, by practicing good judgment. But, how does one get good judgment? Typically, by experience. But, how does one get the experience? Usually, through poor judgment....

I have violated the tact principle so many times, that if I had a dollar for every failure, I would match the government's inflation. Well, not actually, but you get the point....

In any event, there is no substitute for courage and experience in developing tact. [What's needed is the] courage to engage in crucial conversations and...learn from the experience.

Normally, when people have to deal with truth, they are uncomfortable and let their emotions get the best of them. Instead of sharing the truth in love, this comes off as a personal attack on the other party....Simply stated, if the leader damages the relationship, he has lost the ability to influence and it doesn't matter how much truth he has to share.

Therefore, before I enter into any situation where tact is required, I remind myself to never share more truth than the person has the ability to handle. Each person, in a word, has a capacity for truth like a cup has a capacity for liquid. Thus, when a person pours more truth than a person can handle, it's like pouring too much coffee into a cup. In effect, the attempted helpful action—sharing truth—has become offensive because "truth coffee" has spilled all over the person and burned the other person....

> **"A person does not need to be a leadership guru to develop tact."**
> **—Orrin Woodward**

A person does not need to be a leadership guru to develop tact. In fact, every person needs tact in order to influence. Nonetheless, some people live their entire lives violating the principles of tact, burning their most valuable relationships with too much "truth coffee." Indeed, knowing the truth, although important, isn't sufficient. Above all, a leader and mentor must learn to share truth with tact, building relationships and influence with others on his journey to leadership excellence.

To sum up with another very often heard maxim, "People don't care how much you know until they know how much you care," which leads us to...

13

WISDOM

Great mentors are wise mentors. In fact, when we think of the ideal mentor, we naturally imagine or think of someone who has wisdom to impart.

The book *From Smart to Wise* teaches that being smart isn't enough. Top leaders and mentors must seek and use wisdom. Indeed, people will naturally seek out wise leaders and follow their mentoring.

The authors suggested the following tips to becoming wise:

- Be authentic.
- Act appropriately.
- Find and follow your noble purpose.
- Clarify decisions with logic, but decide with discernment.
- Learn when to stand firm and when to be flexible.[12]

Wise leaders and mentors do a few things differently than others. For example, they see the big picture, they understand priorities, and they listen.

Together, these things help them see the right choices in situations where leaders focused on being smart tend to look for the best choice. What's right is almost always more important, and in fact better, than "the best." Sometimes what seems like the best choice is wrong for some reason or another. Wise mentors understand the importance of choosing the *right* things, no matter how many other *good* choices are available.

14

COURTESY

Francis Bacon said, "If a man be gracious and courteous to strangers, it shows he is a citizen of the world."[13] Good mentors know that to be truly effective leaders, they must be courteous, respectful, and considerate of others, whether friend or stranger.

People who disregard the importance of courtesy often present themselves to the world as self-absorbed, closed-minded, and ignorant. This kind of image tends to limit the opportunities a mentor gets to really influence the people he needs to. First impressions matter, and a discourteous person generally doesn't make a very good one.

On the other hand, courteous people present themselves as gracious, humble, and noble. This kind of first impression makes a very positive impact on the people such a mentor meets, and she is able to form important connections and relationships because she was willing to make the small effort to treat people courteously.

Courteous behavior frequently opens doors for mentors and increases their sphere of influence. But the principle goes a level deeper.

Thomas J. Watson said, "Really big people are, above everything else, courteous, considerate, and generous—not just to some people in some circumstances, but to everyone all the time." Mentors should be courteous to others, not only because it increases their chances of future success, but because good mentors seek to be excellent people.

Courtesy is one of the marks of a classy person. Mentors should be looking and working toward their dreams with every action because they know that's how they can succeed over time, but they also need to cultivate the traits of greatness in themselves right now. Every time a mentor is courteous, she achieves a little piece of success by being an outstanding individual.

> **Being responsible for the way we treat others is one of the most important steps to self-mastery and personal excellence.**

As Malcolm S. Forbes put it, "You can easily judge the character of a man by how he treats those who can do nothing for him." An excellent leader treats everyone with respect and generosity, not because he hopes to gain something from each person he ever meets but because he hopes to become something himself. It's not about what he wants from others or what they deserve from him. It's about what he expects from himself.

Being responsible for the way we treat others is one of the most important steps to self-mastery and personal excellence, and because these are both essential to success, conscious and responsible courtesy to others is an important step on the path to achieving lasting success.

Now it is important for mentors and leaders to remember that courtesy is not the only important quality. In fact, there are many others, and people who try to implement just courtesy will likely compromise other important things, and probably even their dreams.

> **Mentors who achieve real success almost never do it by hiding their ideals and dreams from everyone.**

Real leaders know that sometimes they need to stand for an opinion, even at the price of "manners." They understand that being courteous doesn't mean having no opinion; it means being respectful and gracious to others, even if they have a different opinion.

Mentors who achieve real success almost never do it by hiding their ideals and dreams from everyone, on the off chance that somebody might not like what they have to say. No, they do it by having big dreams and sharing them—and by never compromising their principles. But this does not mean they have to be rude or inconsiderate of others.

Mentors should understand and develop this important trait. Doing so will help them increase their influence and multiply their personal triumphs and overall success.

15

READ THE MENTOR'S BOOK

At a meeting of top-performing leaders, a speaker told the following story:

> I know a lot of you are speakers, and I wonder how many of you have ever had the same experience I did several months ago at a convention in Los Angeles. After I finished my speech, I shook hands with several of the attendees and talked to a few others. There was a short break before the next speaker, so a number of people wanted to talk.
>
> Two young men stayed while I finished talking to others in line and then followed me out into the concourse when the event began again. I could see that they were determined to talk to me, so I stopped walking and turned to shake their hands. The first man gave me his card and asked if I would

be willing to e-mail him and perhaps mentor him. He shared his big dreams of becoming a leader and assured me that he was moved by my speech and felt I would be his ideal mentor.

Of course, this happens a lot, so I asked him a question I always ask in such situations. "Have you read my book? If so, what part of it do you need to work on the most?"

He looked at me blankly and then said that he hadn't afforded my book yet. I told him to read my book and follow the suggestions as they applied to him, since I had worked very hard to fill the book with my best mentoring messages.

He seemed disappointed, and I knew that he didn't really want my mentoring. He wanted my connections, not my wisdom.

After he left, the second man stepped forward. He mentioned a section of my book, told me he had been trying to apply it for several months, and asked me how he could improve his success. I immediately wanted to help him because he clearly had done his best to apply my ideas and now needed some personal help to go to the next level.

> I immediately wanted to help him because he clearly had done his best to apply my ideas and now needed some personal help to go to the next level.

I asked for his e-mail address, and the next week, I e-mailed him and helped him work through his questions. I ended up mentoring him for a long time, and each time I gave him a suggestion, he put it to action and only called me back when he was ready to take a new step.

"How many of you have had both of these types of experiences with people as you speak and teach?" he asked the crowd. When almost everyone raised their hand and laughed, he continued:

Of course you have. We all have. And it's sad really because the first type of person could do just as well as the second if he'd try, but it's almost always the second type who really succeeds.

So, as you know, if someone asks for your mentoring, find out if they've already tried. Have they read your book or listened to a speech you've given? If so, have they put it into action? If not, they're probably not ready to be mentored.

Orrin Woodward said, "I have three great books I want to write in my life. I won't talk about all of them right now, but the first one is *RESOLVED* because I filled that book with everything I would teach anyone I mentor. I didn't hold back at all. If anyone asks me to mentor them, I tell them to read *RESOLVED*, to study every word, because that's my mentoring wisdom. Those who do that, who really go through it over and over and learn from it, have been mentored, and then maybe I can help them even more with personalized mentoring."

Mentors should use this guideline when they are approached by individuals seeking mentoring. A good mentor's time is not unlimited, and he should be willing to say no to those who aren't willing to do their part to really achieve success.

It is also important to recognize that good mentors are also good protégés. Before seeking the help and guidance of their own mentors, leaders should make sure they're doing their part to make the most of the mentor's time and effort, rather than wasting it.

16

HOW TO USE ARCHETYPES

Psychologist Carl Jung taught that an important part of our subconscious mind is what he called our "collective unconscious." Unlike the personal subconscious, which stores memories of our own unique experiences, the collective unconscious is a reservoir

> **One of the best ways to organize and understand this collective unconscious—and to understand the people we mentor— is archetypes.**

of common human experience that helps us relate to members of the human family from our own time and from ages past. One of the best ways to organize and understand this collective unconscious—and to understand the people we mentor—is archetypes.

Universal archetypes include such iconic roles as leaders, warriors, inventors, creators, entrepreneurs taking great risks for worthy goals, heroes saving maidens in distress, rescuers, great fathers and mothers, healers, and young lovers. There are many others. Below is a list of common archetypes[14]:

Abuser	Assassin	Comrade
Actor	Avenger	⚹ Coward
Addict	Beggar	Critic
Adonis	Black Widow	Destroyer
Advocate	Boss	Disciple
Alchemist	Bully	Dreamer
Amateur	Caretaker	Drifter
Amazon	Casanova	Elder
Ambassador	Charlatan	Enchantress
Analyst	Chef	Explorer
Angel	Child	Father
Architect	Clown	Flit
Artisan	Companion	Friend

Gambler	Master	Pirate
Glutton	Matriarch	Poet
Goddess	Mediator	Preacher
Guide	✗✗Mentor TO 8H TEENS	Prodigal
Guru	Mercenary	Prince
Healer	Merchant	Princess
Hedonist	Messiah	Prophet
Herald	Midas	Puppet
Hermit	Minister	Queen
Hero	Miser	Rabbi
Heroine	Monk	Rock Star
Icon	Monster	Ruler in Exile
Innocent	Mother	Savior
Inventor	Mystic	Scholar
Judge	Nomad	Seeker
King	Nun	Seer
Knight	Nurse	Servant
Leader	Nymph	Shaman
Legislator	Olympian	Shape Shifter
Liberator	Oracle	Siren
Loser	Orphan	Slave
Lover	Patriarch	Sleuth
Magician	Pilgrim	Soldier
Martyr	Pioneer	Spy

Stepchild	Traitor	Weaver
Steward	Trickster	Widow
Storyteller	Tutor	Wizard
Student	Vampire	Workaholic
Teacher	Victim	Wounded Child
Tease	Visionary	Wounded Healer
Temptress	Wanderer	
Thief	Warrior	

WORKSHOP

Read through the list of archetypes—get to know it. Now, read through it again, and underline any archetype that feels like "you." (You may want to make copies first, so you can use this list with your mentees.) Mark anything you identify with.

When you've done that, go through the list again and narrow it down to the ten that are most like you.

Next, go through your list of ten and mark the one that is really the very most like you.

Finally, pick the one that you most *want* to fit you. When you've done this for yourself, repeat the process on a new copy for each of your mentees.

Knowing this about yourself and your protégé(s) will help you understand each other and your dreams. It will also help you to plot the best course to achieving those dreams.

17

Tenacity Trumps Talent

William Shakespeare wrote, "Some are born great, some achieve greatness, and others have greatness thrust upon them."[15] Some English scholars have suggested that Shakespeare meant this as a joke, but the statement rings true regardless of whether he said it in jest or seriousness. Greatness comes in many forms and in many circumstances. However, the quote, while obviously true, is deceiving in one way: In truth, all great mentors (and people) are that way because they achieved it.

Everyone who has become a wise and effective mentor has had to work hard, make mistakes, learn from successes and failures, and earn his or her wisdom. Excellent mentoring is the natural result of learning the important lessons of life and then caring enough to help others learn them as well. Whether he was born great or had it thrust upon him, every great mentor had to pursue a challenging path of self-improvement.

> **Excellent mentoring is the natural result of learning the important lessons of life and then caring enough to help others learn them as well.**

The good news for many people is that if they were not born great, and didn't even have greatness thrust upon them, they can still achieve greatness. The key is not to focus on becoming great but rather to do the small and simple things that naturally bring great results. Those who do so tenaciously, never giving up, often become great.

Tenacity brings talent, over time. Talent can never replace tenacity.

A person who is really trying is going to have much better long-term results than a person who is not. As in the fable of the tortoise and the hare, no amount of natural talent will win you the race if you're napping while the other guy is steadily giving it his all. And more to the point, you aren't in a race with anyone except yourself.

Your success as a mentor, a leader, and a person is limited (or liberated) by the size of your dream and the dedication you put toward it. To succeed, you must know who you are, where you are, and where you want to be and then make it happen. Knowing your dream is a vital part of any significant progress.

As you meet potential protégés, remember that a gifted person who waits around to be chosen for greatness will probably never really be great at anything, while a resolute person who chooses greatness and tenaciously acts to bring it about will almost certainly find it. That said, mentors should search out mentees who exhibit tenacity, even more than those with natural talent, and then teach their protégés how central hard work and perseverance are to success.

Tenacity trumps talent, or, as Shakespeare put it, "Though she be but little, she is fierce."

18

CHOOSING TO BE ALL IN

Part of being a tenacious mentor is choosing to be "all in." As long as a mentor is holding back on the sidelines, he is not working hard enough, or perhaps he just isn't fully invested yet. Great mentors make the choice and jump in.

One of the most common reasons for not going all in is fear of failure. Rosalynn Carter said, "You must accept that you might fail; then, if you do your

> **Successful mentors move beyond the fear of appearing the fool or the failure.**

best and still don't win, at least you can be satisfied that you've tried. If you don't accept failure as a possibility, you don't set high goals, you don't branch out, you don't try—you don't take the risk."

Refusing to go all in based on fear of failure is sad enough, but, as Orrin Woodward wrote in his book *RESOLVED*, in many cases people actually fear the appearance of failure more than failure itself. This can be tragic, and at the very least, it is more than a little bit silly.

Successful mentors move beyond the fear of appearing the fool or the failure. Entrepreneur Jim Rohn said, "If you are not willing to risk the unusual, you will have to settle for the ordinary." A mentor who is willing to look silly when necessary is nearly always more relatable, inspiring, and effective than a mentor who is limited by his need to fit in or never take wise risks.

Another thing that stops people from going all in is the fear of working hard. Every great mentor has learned that achieving great things naturally requires hard work. That's part of the bargain, but it is so worth it. Martin Luther King Jr. said, "All labor that uplifts humanity has dignity and importance and should be undertaken with painstaking excellence."

Mentors who accept the call to greatness will have joy along with their work. As Confucius put it, "Choose a job you love, and you will never have to work a day in your life."

The decision to go all in is only the beginning, but it will make a huge difference in the success and happiness of people who want to be superb mentors—and help them set an example for their protégés to emulate.

Naturally, if a mentor's commitment goes unmet by the mentee, the process will break down, but as good mentors do what it takes on their side of the relationship and help mentees to learn and implement this principle, they will be able to achieve higher levels of success than if they attempted to go at it with half-hearted drive and enthusiasm.

If you agree to mentor someone, go all in!

19

DON'T MISTAKE THINKING FOR ACTION

The idea of "choosing to be all in" from the last chapter presents a common pitfall: thinking the choice was all it took. Often mentors and mentees think that because they're having big thoughts, considering big dreams, or "deciding" on big futures, they are becoming big successes. This is not true.

Thinking and planning are vital, but success requires action. It is important to choose to take the journey and to decide you'll follow it to its end, but you must also *start walking*.

The story is told of a young man who went to a week-long leadership mentoring conference. He attended speeches and workshops every day and heard from several top leaders and mentors on subjects ranging from business leadership to parent-mentoring to self-knowledge/-love. Even mealtimes were filled with exciting discussions about topics that were meaningful to him. He interacted with people who shared his ideals and desire to become an excellent mentor. All in all, he had a truly inspirational and motivating week.

When he got home, he couldn't wait to get on the phone with his own mentor; he was sure she was going to love what he had to tell her!

"It was so amazing!" he said when his mentor asked about the event. "It totally changed my life."

"Really? That's great. How?"

"Well, it was just so inspiring. I learned all these cool principles and thought of things in new ways that had never occurred to me before. I just feel so pumped about it all. It was a real life-changer, no joke." The young man's voice was full of excitement.

> **Thinking and planning are vital, but success requires action.**

"That's fantastic! Experiences like that can be hugely motivating," the mentor replied enthusiastically. "Having new ideas and meeting with a bunch of people who share your goals can really energize a person. But how did it change your life? Let me say it differently: How will it change the way you *live* your life? How will you *act* differently?"

"Hmm. Good question."

He pondered for a few minutes until she cut him off. "The last thing I want is to ruin your excitement with my pragmatism. The excitement isn't enough just on its own, but you'll definitely need it if the process I have in mind is going to work."

They began brainstorming ways for him to implement the things he had learned—how to turn an inspiring impression into an actual life change. The things he had gained from the seminar had the potential to change his life but only if he could find the right ways to enact them and then actually follow through.

His mentor guided him, using his excitement to motivate action. They soon discovered that he knew what improvements he wanted to see in himself and even some of the first steps to getting there. His mentor helped him understand that the big thoughts are great, as long as they lead to big action—or, even more important, the small actions that bring big results.

This principle is one of the most important for every mentor to know because it is often the difference between great realities and merely big dreams.

It also applies to the way the mentor deals with his own ideas regarding his mentees. A mentor knows that until he acts on his impressions of what his mentee needs, those thoughts won't do much to help the mentee. Thoughts must be developed until they present decent avenues for * action. Then they should be acted upon.

Wise planning precedes effective action, and taking action is required for progress. Good mentors will steer the protégé's big ideas and high ideals into specific action.

*WHY AM I STILL HAVING TO LEARN THIS!

20

DON'T MISTAKE ACTION FOR RESULTS

One of the great historical mentors whose ideas have inspired many people is Buddha. For example, he said, "There are two mistakes one can make along the road to truth...not going all the way, and not starting." We've already discussed the second mistake, not starting, and how taking action is essential to success. Now let's talk about the first mistake: not finishing.

Thinking and acting are very important, but in the end, mentors are looking for something better: results. In fact, their mentees are actually seeking the same thing, whether they realize it or not.

Good mentors are constantly transforming thoughts into actions. They know that success requires them to take things into their own hands, rather than waiting for circumstances to change on their own. However, if they get too caught up in what they're *doing*, it is possible for them to miss what they're not *accomplishing*.

Being busy doesn't mean you are actually getting the right things done. Mentors must always be aware not only of what they're doing but of what results they're achieving. The key to making your tenacity bring success is to make sure it's working in the right direction. Effective mentors constantly check their results, and when they find the wrong ones, they reconsider their course of action.

Just as thinking is really valuable only if it leads to action, action is really beneficial only if it leads to positive results. And while unexpected or undesirable results can teach great lessons (as we'll discuss later), ultimately the goal is to achieve positive results. That said, if a mentor sees that his actions, or his protégé's actions, are producing negative results, it's time to switch things up.

> **Being busy doesn't mean you are actually getting the right things done.**

Einstein defined insanity as doing the same thing over and over and expecting different results. When the course of action is failing, recognize it and get a new one. Don't strain relationships or continue to waste time and resources by repeating failing methods. On the flip side, if an action is achieving great results, recognize that as well! It should be celebrated and continued.

Recognizing both failures and successes will help mentors improve their ability to influence their protégés, and it can also strengthen the relationship between them. Praising positive results and correcting negative action in wise and tactful ways is one of the most effective tools of building trust and respect in a mentorship bond.

As Larry Bossidy and Ram Charan have suggested, "If you want to know how you're doing as a leader, just look at how well the people you lead are doing."[16]

21

HOW (AND WHEN) TO PRAISE

Once mentees have set goals and started acting toward desired results, mentors should be constantly watching for opportunities to praise good performance and success. Recognizing and celebrating progress builds love and trust in the relationship, making it easier for parties to communicate goals, concerns, and anything else.

In their book *The One-Minute Manager*, Kenneth Blanchard and Spencer Johnson outlined the steps of a good "praising":

1. Let people know in advance that you'll be giving them input on how they're doing.

2. Praise people immediately. Catch them doing something right, and let them know.

3. Be specific in your praise—they should know exactly what you're praising them for.

4. Tell them how good you feel about what they've done right, how proud you are, and how their actions and results will positively impact their lives and the world around them.

5. Give them a few moments of silence to *feel* their rightness.

6. Encourage them to keep it up.[17]

Mentors who look for situations to praise the positive results and actions of their mentees will increase their own influence and effectiveness as well as the performance of those with whom they work.

To illustrate this principle, one mentor shared the following story:

A young writer timidly approached the door with a short piece she was considering for publication. It was something they had been talking about for a while, but she still wasn't sure she was ready. After turning back three times, she finally worked up the courage to knock on his door. It wasn't that she was scared of him, not really. But once he had seen the paper, she couldn't pretend she hadn't written anything yet.

"Come in," he said.

She opened the door and walked in.

Her mentor smiled when he saw the two-page document, and she tried to look as nonchalant as possible. "Hey, it's good to see you," he said. "What can I do for you?"

"Well, I finally wrote this piece. I was wondering if you might take a look at it...?"

She fidgeted as he silently read, watching him for any sign of disapproval, or worse—amusement.

Finally, he looked up. *What is he going to say? Oh no, I shouldn't have brought it to him. It's just stupid. I should stick to proofreading, or—*

"This is brilliant."

"What?" She couldn't quite believe it.

"This is really, really good. When did you write this?"

"Um, I've been working on it all week. Just finished an hour ago."

"Well, I'm really pleased with it. You're really progressing. I love the tone you've chosen, and your references are perfect! Very artistic and moving piece. It's really well written."

"Thanks." She beamed.

"I think you should make it longer. It's so good, I found myself wanting more. Do you think you could write a few more pages on this topic?"

"Sure. Yeah, that sounds fun. Do you have any tips for me?"

He took her through the paper and pointed out a few places where the word choice or the order could be better, and she walked out of the room filled with ideas on how to improve her article.

> **Appropriate praise leads to abundant progress and paves the way for proper correction.**

She came back several times throughout the week to show him what she had done with it. Each time she returned, she was more confident, and the quality of her writing improved.

As she received praise for work well done, she became more willing to try new things and express new ideas. Their relationship became more open, and he was able to teach her much more because she was willing to be herself. When she knew he'd be honest and free with his praise, the dread of his displeasure became smaller and smaller. She trusted him to be honest and loving.

As she became more daring, she began to truly excel.

Mentors who recognize achievement and give proper praise and encouragement inspire trust and hard work in their protégés. And when a mentee knows she has been rightly praised, she is more likely to receive reprimands in the same positive spirit, and recognize their place in her success.

Appropriate praise leads to abundant progress and paves the way for proper correction.

22

HOW (AND WHEN) TO REPRIMAND

Chris Brady and Orrin Woodward wrote, "When mentoring, it's a leader's job to identify where the protégé is off track and provide correction to get him back on track."[18] They went on to list several questions a mentor should ask herself in order to help her protégé past his blind spots, problems, or weaknesses and to emphasize his best traits.

1. What principles is the protégé missing?
2. What are his thinking patterns? How are they wrong?
3. How can the protégé see things differently so he can behave and perform more effectively?
4. How are his attitudes inappropriate or unproductive?
5. What is he missing that he needs to see, and how can I help him find it?

Mentors frequently find that their mentees have difficulty with this process. It's often hard to recognize one's own failings and weaknesses; that's why they're called blind spots. And this is why it's helpful for mentors to step in and help their mentees confront their areas of weakness. Such corrections should be handled with love. If the protégé is questioning whether his mentor really has his best interests in mind, he will likely be more defensive and less willing to actually change. He must know that his mentor wouldn't intentionally hurt him.

In their book *The New Tolerance*, Josh McDowell and Bob Hostetler said that mentors need to speak with "humble truth and aggressive love." This means that the truth is communicated in such a way that the mentee doesn't feel demoralized by it, and the love is communicated so strongly throughout the encounter that he doesn't have to get offended or defensive.

This gives the protégé the opportunity to really work on the problem without risking the relationship. Mentors should be on their guard to be certain they don't reverse the two and rain down upon mentees with "aggressive truth and humble love," as Brady and Woodward put it.

Humble truth means being honest and direct. Tell the mentee where he messed up and how to fix it. And do the whole thing in a spirit of aggressive love.

It is essential that mentors remember that once the reprimand is over, it is over. Past wrongdoings or mistakes should not be continually rehashed or brought up. Once an issue is resolved, it should be dropped. Bringing up past problems after they are resolved and fixed hurts trust and makes mentees feel defensive rather than open to correction.

Reprimands that are done well, just like well-timed praisings, can be wonderful bonding experiences and great teaching opportunities.

23

CONFLICT RESOLUTION

The harder the conflict, the more glorious the triumph.
— THOMAS PAINE

One of the most important parts of being a mentor is learning how to effectively deal with conflict. Many times you will discover a disagreement between people you work with or are mentoring, and too often it is left alone until it builds into a problem. This can make the conflict much bigger than if you had handled it correctly when it first arose.

As a mentor, when you notice a problem, deal with it immediately. Set up a meeting with the people directly involved in the conflict. Don't invite outsiders to throw in their opinions and muddle everything, just the people who are emotionally invested and truly a part of the problem—and the solution.

Begin the meeting with prayer, and invite the people to talk about their concerns. Lay down the ground rules, and don't be afraid to set boundaries for the conversation:

instruct participants to be courteous and civil, focus on the problem at hand, and so forth.

Allow everyone to get their main points out, encourage opposing parties to see the other side of the issue, and look for common ground. Give everyone a chance to speak and suggest how they would solve things if they were on the other side of the table.

> **As a mentor, when you see a problem, deal with it immediately.**

Stay positive and focused on understanding each other and finding solutions.

Try to avoid being swayed emotionally. You are there to help the other people work through their concerns and establish shared, meaningful plans to fix them.

Good mentors face conflict directly and follow these basic guidelines.

24

TURNING "FAILURE" INTO PROGRESS

Henry Ford said, "Failure is simply the opportunity to begin again, this time more intelligently." This is an excellent way for leaders and mentors to see failure—as an opportunity. View failure as a chance to look over your notes, fix your calculations, and make a fresh start.

For example, Thomas Edison said, "After we had conducted thousands of experiments on a certain project without solving the problem, one of my associates, after we had conducted the crowning experiment and it had proved a failure, expressed discouragement and disgust over our having failed to find out anything. I cheerily assured him that we had learned something. For we had learned for a certainty that the thing couldn't be done that way, and that we would have to try some other way."[19]

Mentors should also see failure as an excellent learning opportunity and teach their mentees to do the same. Malcolm Forbes said, "Failure is success, if we learn from it." Whatever the reason for failure (lack of preparation, lack of dedication, lack of information, lack of vision, etc.), it can be used to teach some pretty big lessons—often about the very thing that caused the failure: the importance of preparation, dedication, information, vision, and so forth.

Failure is a natural consequence of *doing*. Everyone who ever accomplished anything great had his or her share of failures along the way. Failure can be many things to many people, just like success. It can be an opportunity or a lesson or even a little break, but what it should never be is an excuse to blame others, to stop trying, or to give up. Perhaps Denis Waitley put it best when he said, "Failure should be our teacher, not our undertaker.

"Failure is delay, not defeat. It is a temporary detour, not a dead end. Failure is something we can avoid only by saying nothing, doing nothing, and being nothing."

When we fail, we need to learn from it—then pick

> **Failure is a natural consequence of *doing*.**

ourselves up and take action. Mentors who understand this know that failure is just one of the steps to success, so they take it, dissect it, and discover where they went wrong.

The course correction questions from the chapter on reprimands are an excellent place to start for dealing with personal failures. Specifically, ask yourself:

1. What principles am I missing?
2. What are my thinking patterns? How are they wrong?
3. How can I see things differently so I can behave and perform more effectively?
4. How are my attitudes inappropriate or unproductive?
5. What am I not seeing that I need to see? What must I do (or whose help do I need) to see the whole picture?

Since a mentor's failure very often impacts the people he serves, he should add another question to his list when dealing with personal mistakes:

6.   Is there anyone I have hurt or damaged by my failure with whom I need to make things right?

Once these questions are answered, mentors immediately get to work on implementing their solutions. Just as in dealing with protégés, mentors should approach personal failure with aggressive love. It's not about *beating* yourself up; it's about *gearing* yourself up to begin again with renewed eagerness and drive.

Personal course corrections, when done right, can be very cleansing and inspiring and should lead to higher productivity and more rewarding work.

> **It's not about beating yourself up; it's about gearing yourself up!**

Mentors who approach their own mistakes and failures in this way are more likely to be effective in helping their mentees learn these same lessons. Everybody has setbacks. Strong leaders turn them into important launching pads to success.

25

KEEP HUMOR IN YOUR MENTORING

Comedian Yakov Smirnoff said, "Everybody laughs the same in every language, because laughter is a universal connection." Practically every mentor-to-protégé relationship will benefit from closeness, trust, genuine friendship, and positive energy. An unapproachable mentor generally doesn't have the optimal connection with her mentees.

The best communication flows both ways. While mentors may give assignments, praise, and correction, their mentees should feel comfortable bringing questions, ideas, goals, and concerns to their mentors.

Many beginning mentors worry that being humorous or personal with their mentees will destroy their mystique and undermine their authority. While this idea has some truth, it is really irrelevant in the long term because making the relationship more personal will tend to help mentees relax, listen, and learn more effectively.

Humor tends to make the mentee less afraid of his mentor, especially at the beginning of the relationship. Despite the teachings of Machiavelli (who placed fear above feeling in relational authority), a mentor who has the trust of her mentees is usually able to do more for them than one who is feared.

The use of appropriate humor allows mentees to respect their mentor for her real, genuine superiorities—the things she has to teach them, the wisdom they have yet to gain, and so forth—rather than the nominal or bureaucratic superiority of being "in charge." The best mentors, those with respectable qualities and experience, do not have to rely on position, title, intimidation, or aloofness to retain the respect of their mentees.

Appropriate use of humor will not interfere with the right kind of respect. It will merely help to remove the obstacles of reservation and insecurity, and it is an excellent way to open up the flow of two-way communication.

There is yet a deeper level to this. E. E. Cummings said that "the most wasted of all days is one without humor." Laughter is more than just an excellent tool; it is also the expression of joy and friendship, which should be felt and experienced every day. Orrin Woodward listed friendship as one of the most important of thirteen resolutions for leaders.

The relationship between mentor and protégé can be mutually rewarding on levels beyond what each learns from the other. Mentors shouldn't take themselves too seriously. Life, with all its hard work and big dreams, is still supposed to be fun! They should take the mission seriously, but help achieve it with smiles and enjoyment.

Laughter is a great part of friendship, and great mentors should cultivate genuine and fulfilling friendships with their mentees. In his timeless essay "The Inner Ring," C. S. Lewis reminded us that real friendship, based on mutual affection, is one of the Aristotelian virtues and causes a good "half of the happiness in the world."

As psychologist William James said, "We don't laugh because we're happy; we're happy because we laugh."

With all that said, it should be noted that Aristotle, C. S. Lewis, and William James were three of the least comical people ever.

26

INSPIRE

One of the most important principles of excellent mentoring is "inspire, not require."[20] People who do something because they feel strongly that they want to do it are more likely to be effective than people who do it just because it was "assigned," and they almost always learn more from the doing.

Mentors who instill a sense of personal conviction in their mentees get better results than those who merely get them to do their "homework" because people who have a clear vision of what needs to be done and a strong desire to work hard to achieve it tend to accomplish much more than people who sit around waiting to be given a task. In fact, too often the latter group tends to work at the bare minimum level.

Being an inspiring mentor means helping mentees capture a vision and allowing them to tenaciously fight for it because they want to, not because they have to. An inspired person works harder and gets more done than a merely required person.

It's easy to see how helpful this can be in many aspects of business, where the goal is productivity and efficiency, but when it comes to mentoring, inspiration rises above mere helpfulness. Mentors are looking for more than just

95

high production; their goal is the real growth and learning of their mentee—the long-term production.

A great mentor is trying to shape more great mentors. In order to achieve this, he must bring his mentees' search for truth to a conscious level. They shouldn't be dependent on him for their drive, and the goal shouldn't be merely to not anger him, or even to please him; it should be about their dream for themselves.

In reality, this is another example of the power and importance of tenacity. As mentors and protégés become more conscious of their hopes and dreams, the need and opportunity for demonstrating real tenacity becomes more prominent.

> **Mentors are looking for more than just high production; their goal is the real growth and learning of their mentee—the long-term production.**

"Inspire, not require" means that the mentor will give his mentee the reins on her production and growth. He will help her understand that she holds the power to either fail miserably or succeed greatly—as he offers help and guidance along the way.

Of course, mentors should be so inspiring that the mentee really believes in what she's doing—she should know how much it matters and be ready to give it a good fight. But the fight must be hers. If she works simply to put a checkmark on his list, she will not fulfill her greatest potential.

An excellent example of this is the mentoring style of Atticus Finch in *To Kill a Mockingbird*. With his children, he creates an environment of constant self-improvement. He tells them enough that they understand and appreciate everything he shows them, but his mentoring style is primarily show, not tell; inspire, not require.

A mentor who understands this principle knows that the question "Why?" is one of his best friends. It offers the opportunity to provide the explanation that gives his constant example context, taking it from random action to inspiring drive. He must remember, however, that effective inspiration requires more than just action and example; the explanation *is* necessary.

A mentor who ignores her mentee and just does her own thing, expecting to really inspire him, will probably be disappointed. The mentee will often feel snubbed and have a hard time recognizing any example because he's too caught up in wondering why his mentor threw him off. But if she has made herself clear, and he knows what she's fighting for, her vehemence will boost his own.

It is true that in business, in mentoring, and in life, the right kind of requiring holds an important place. But just as talent cannot really win without tenacity, requirement cannot be its best without inspired dedication to it.

An inspiring mentor has big dreams and helps his mentees to catch their own big dreams. And then, by example, he demonstrates how to fight for them with everything they've got.

27

THE POWER OF EXAMPLE

The example a mentor sets will often make or break her credibility and effectiveness. No amount of well-intentioned talking is going to rescue a situation where the example is blatantly contrary to the teachings. If a protégé manages to succeed and excel despite an unreliable mentor, his tenacity is to be commended, but his mentor is not.

Francis Bacon wrote, "He that gives good advice, builds with one hand; he that gives good counsel and example, builds with both; but he that gives good admonition and bad example, builds with one hand and pulls down with the other."

> **"Few things are harder to put up with than the annoyance of a good example."**
> **—Mark Twain**

A positive example can give mentees the inspiration to fight for big dreams, but a negative one can make them question whether the big dreams are even worth fighting for. In fact, negative example not only discounts the value of positive words and big talk, but it also tends to damage the ability of the mentee to fully engage in future mentor relationships because he gets into bad habits and fosters incorrect thought patterns for as long as he remains in an unproductive situation.

Thus, a mentor's bad example not only pulls down the things she's trying to build, but it also makes it harder for future mentors to pick up the pieces she leaves behind.

On the flip side, positive example is one of the most powerful motivators. Mark Twain wrote, "Few things are harder to put up with than the annoyance of a good example."[21] This quote is clearly dripping with Twain's customary irony, but it makes an excellent point.

Good people, with good hopes and dreams and a good understanding of the situation, generally find it particularly difficult to "put up" with a good example without trying

> **Great mentors start by being great people.**

to follow it. A mentor who continuously dangles an excellent example in front of her mentee's face often succeeds in making him bite.

Great mentors start by being great people. They focus on being who they should be and want to be, and accomplishing what they want to accomplish. As mentees watch their mentor, and gain respect and appreciation for how hard she works to be successful and how happy it makes her to do her best, they will feel more and more inspired to emulate her strengths.

As was mentioned in an earlier chapter, when mentoring, it is better to *show* than to *tell*. A mentor should let her protégé *see* the right way of doing things, not just tell him about it. Of course, everyone makes mistakes. Even a great mentor will not have perfect success in everything she ever tries. But the great thing is, even in her failures, her example can be an inspiration to her mentees.

As her mentees see her persistently trying to achieve greatness—sometimes stumbling, but *always* picking herself back up—they will feel empowered and eager to do the same. And as they see the joy and fulfillment she gets from the results of her hard work, they will learn to want it for themselves.

28

HERO MENTORS

The most unlikely of nobodies comes from a small town in the middle of nowhere. Strange circumstances take him from his home and throw him into some conflict that has the future of the world hanging in the balance. Somehow, it is up to him to save us all.

He meets many friends along his path, and they each have something special to teach him about himself, life, or the world. In the end, when the conflict comes to its peak, he finds that he is uniquely qualified (because of who he is, where he comes from, and what he's been through) to come up with a crazy solution that will make everything right in the universe. So, with God's help, he does.

From the epic poems of ancient Greece to westerns, from Plutarch's histories to the modern sci-fi/fantasy genre, hero stories (all of which, more or less, follow the above progression) have been among the most influential movers of society. Even before written history, tribes told and retold stories in oral traditions. Whole communities gathered around campfires to hear the latest twist to an old story from the best storytellers.

Today we read books or gather around movie screens to do the same. Even those who think television is a waste of time frequently listen to audios or attend speeches where top corporate leaders tell the latest inspiring story.

> **Many mentors will find that some variation of this story is exactly the one that ought to be told of each of their mentees.**

The story of the unlikely hero saving the world is repeated in all sorts of art and literature, as well as plain old history, and it could be called the most popular of storylines. However, many mentors will find that some variation of this story is exactly the one that ought to be told of each of their mentees.

That said, each of the mentees could certainly benefit from hearing it a few times, with the express purpose of finding their own hero-mentors.

Hero-mentors can include historical figures, literary characters, or anyone worthy of admiration and emulation. A mentor who teaches his mentees to learn the lessons best taught by hero-mentors helps them take advantage of the vast reservoir of human knowledge, instead of relying solely on his own limited experience.

With hero-mentors in place, when a mentee comes to a crossroads in life, when she has to make a decision she's never faced before, she has more than her own life and her mentor's to help her; she can think about what Joan of Arc would do. How would Margaret Thatcher handle this? When Jane Eyre was faced with a similar decision, what was *her* reaction?

Everyone who wants to be a leader can learn from studying George Washington, William Wilberforce, or Tecumseh. Whoever your heroes are, learn from them. And help your protégés do the same.

Just as people can be inspired and taught by the example of their mentors, they can learn from the example of their heroes. Looking to hero-mentors can give inspiration and direction when a mentee doesn't know what to do, comfort and resolve when he has failed, and encouragement to say, "If he did it, so can I!"

For example, reporter Alex Knapp wrote about some important leadership lessons that we can learn from Batman: (1) organizations need to be built around ideas, not people; (2) actions matter more than intentions; (3) trust people with the truth; (4) you need to risk

> **Just as people can be inspired and taught by the example of their mentors, they can learn from the example of their heroes.**

failure in order to succeed; and (5) when you do fail, don't let it destroy you.[22]

Here are just a few of the lessons the life of Mother Teresa can teach her hero-mentees:

"Life is an opportunity, benefit from it.
Life is beauty, admire it.
Life is a dream, realize it.
Life is a challenge, meet it.
Life is a duty, complete it.
Life is a game, play it.
Life is a promise, fulfill it.
Life is sorrow, overcome it.
Life is a song, sing it.
Life is a struggle, accept it.
Life is a tragedy, confront it.
Life is an adventure, dare it.
Life is luck, make it.
Life is too precious, do not destroy it.
Life is life, fight for it."

From Superman, we can learn the importance of never giving up. A person may not have super strength all the time, but he can still tenaciously work for his dreams. Superman always keeps fighting for his cause, no matter what his enemies throw at him. Even when they bring out the kryptonite, which literally cripples him and leaves him writhing on the floor, he keeps going. He never lets anyone take his dreams from him.

He also teaches the importance of being your best self instead of trying to fit in or please everyone. He dreams big and lives accordingly.

Lessons we can learn from Frederick Douglass include resourcefulness, perseverance, the responsibility that comes with power, the importance of reading to success, the value of ignoring those who criticize or discourage, and so forth.

At an even deeper level, a mentor might find the answers he needs for one of his mentees from a hero-mentor of his own. There have been many great mentors throughout history and in literature who have very important lessons to pass on (many have been referenced and quoted in this book). Chris Brady and Orrin Woodward wrote, "Experience is not the best teacher; other people's experience is the best teacher."

One of Woodward's heroes is Vince Lombardi, and many of Orrin's mentees have learned lots about themselves by hearing Orrin talk about Lombardi's contributions. Orrin keeps a picture of the great football coach in the study of his Florida home, and this has led to many conversations about great leadership techniques and beliefs.

Mentors and mentees who want to be great leaders and heroes in the world should study the heroes of the past and learn from them. As the great British politician Benjamin Disraeli wrote, "Nurture your mind with great thoughts. To believe in the heroic makes heroes."

29

SEEING THE GENIUS IN EVERY PERSON

Ralph Waldo Emerson said, "When Nature has work to be done, she creates a genius to do it."[23] Every person in this world has potential genius within and an important work to do.

One of the joys and excitements of mentoring is discovering the particular brand of genius each mentee possesses and finding the best way to bring it out. Of course, it is up to the mentee to do most of this, but mentors can help the process by giving directed and meaningful guidance that matches the needs of the mentee.

It is a great honor to be involved in molding the next generation of great leaders and mentors. Understanding that today's budding genius-mentee has the potential and the mission to become tomorrow's leader—and even hero—will help mentors to both feel the significance of their job and shape the messages they pass on.

> **One of the joys and excitements of mentoring is discovering the particular brand of genius each mentee possesses and finding the best way to bring it out.**

A mentor who is guiding a potential genius and leader (and all mentors are) should stress to his mentee the importance of staying true to herself and her dream. Emerson warned against the threat that society itself poses to genius. He said that bureaucratic or rote conformity often attempts to destroy genius, or at the very least makes its existence irrelevant, by ensuring that it is ever inactive. [24]

A world full of people who worry only about looking good and fitting in is a world where genius goes unnoticed, untapped, and unrewarded.

The problems of the world will never be solved without genius, and the progress of the world will stall without it. Luckily, God and nature do send geniuses, as there is plenty of work to be done. Unfortunately, the genius inside us has been under attack since the beginning of history. That is why the world so desperately needs great mentors who recognize each mentee's genius and help each of them to cultivate it.

30

SEEING YOUR PLACE IN THE BIG PICTURE

Mentors are essential in keeping societies from declining. The forces of decline are real, whether we're discussing Orrin Woodward's Five Laws of Decline or just reading history and seeing the results of negative choices, leaders, and policies. Indeed, the characteristics of decline can be tracked through the centuries.

In *The History of the Decline and Fall of the Roman Empire*, for example, author Edward Gibbon defined five attributes of the Roman Empire at the time of its fall:

1. A mounting love of show and luxury
2. A widening gap between the very rich and the very poor
3. An obsession with sex
4. Freakishness in the arts, masquerading as originality
5. An increased desire to live off the state

Woodward wrote that "even a perfunctory examination of the modern West would reveal it is suffering from a similar cultural decline to that of the Roman Empire. Indeed, a solid argument could be made that the modern West has surpassed Rome in many of its negative influences."

If our generation is going to turn around the current momentum toward decline, the next generation of leaders is going to need a fantastic mentoring force. Today's mentors need to understand that continuing the modern slide of the free world away from principles of morality, family, freedom, and free enterprise is simply not a viable option.

In short, today's mentors are training the coming generation of leaders and mentors. At a time like this, now more than ever, the world needs dedicated leaders who will settle for nothing less than excellence. E. E. Cummings wrote, "To be nobody-but-yourself—in a world which is doing its best, night and day, to make you everybody else—means to fight the hardest battle which any human being can fight: and never stop fighting."

> **If our generation is going to turn around the current momentum toward decline, the next generation of leaders is going to need a fantastic mentoring force.**

The implication of this statement is that swimming against the cultural current of decline is both necessary and rewarding. Great mentors must train others to be great mentors. It is the only thing that will save a society in decline.

Always keep the reality of this battle in mind. This is a vital technique of effective mentoring in our modern world.

31

GENERATIONS

Good mentors work hard to be good followers of their own mentors. The best mentors are usually those who understand that in order to keep up with the rapid growth of their driven protégés, they also have to be constantly progressing. To continue being helpful, they regularly need to update their stores of knowledge, skill, experience, and especially wisdom.

Mentors should be voracious readers. Consistent reading is one of the keys of success. As was mentioned earlier, familiarity with and immersion in the great books of history is one of the things that can bring a mentor's level of effectiveness from low to exceptionally high. Learning and applying new concepts from reading deep books will refresh a mentor's ideas and revolutionize his thinking. No matter how much experience and background a mentor has, he can always benefit from reading and applying the right kind of new material.

Another way mentors can be good followers of their own mentors is by listening to their advice, speeches, and audio recordings. Having a good audio on hand at all times will help a mentor keep himself in the ambiance of progress and ultimately of success. This is one of the easiest and most effective ways for a mentor to improve his personal progress as well as his success.

Orrin Woodward and Chris Brady wrote, "There is tremendous economy of time to be gained when listening to an audio recording while driving a car, taking a shower, or performing mindless chores." Mentors who understand how much impact this one simple action can have on their lives would be almost foolish *not* to take advantage of it.

Good mentors should also choose their friends and associates carefully. Jim Rohn said, "You are the average of the five people you spend the most time with." Mentors who want to be smashingly successful should surround themselves with people who are smashingly successful, as well as those who also desire to be. A mentor who is on the path to great success is often someone who creates an environment where he can be continuously learning from his friends and colleagues. He should be able to look up to those around him as his mentors in some aspect of life.

Mentors should also be the kind of people who ask questions. Great mentors know how and when to ask the best questions of their mentors, and they patiently wait for needed answers. These questions will sometimes be about their own lives and experiences—things

> **A good mentor will take advantage of her own mentor to find meaningful answers regarding her mentees.**

they need to continue their own progress. However, a good mentor will take advantage of her own mentor to find meaningful answers regarding her mentees.

Good mentors should also be fantastic "grandparent" mentors! As mentioned earlier, this means that they see more than one "generation" down the mentoring line. They should be aware of their mentees' mentees, and so on. A mentor should be prepared to answer a mentee's questions and offer insights about the mentee's mentoring. Ultimately, good mentoring will go beyond one step down the line and influence many more people than just the mentee. So mentors should learn how to learn from their mentors and pass that on in meaningful ways that continue to bless lives long after they utter the final notes of each lesson.

An excellent illustration of the concept of generational mentoring is the idea of a relay race. Relay racing allows individuals to compete in much longer races than they could run on their own. Because runner 1 can pass the baton to runner 2 (who then passes it to runner 3, and so on), the team as a whole finishes the race. Likewise, each generation of mentors is like one of the runners.

Finally, there is no substitute for hard work. Imagine if runner 2 decided he didn't have to work hard because he saw that the people on both sides of him were already planning to work hard themselves. The baton would stop for a lemonade break somewhere between runner 1 and runner 3, and the race would end right then and there for that team. Whatever the focus of the mentor's career, business, or calling, he should mentor the skills of success in his chosen field—and help his mentees do the same.

To summarize, mentors continuously learn from their mentors, and then they pass on what they have been taught. Mentors should make sure their protégés understand this big picture so that they too can optimize their impact and keep passing on important lessons.

32

THE POWER OF FOCUS

Napoleon Hill said, "You can be anything you want to be, if you only believe with sufficient conviction and act in accordance with your faith; for whatever the mind can conceive and believe, the mind can achieve." Mentors who can get their mentees out of the "dabbling" mentality and into the "focused" mind-set will see significant results.

One great mentor said that "the greatest revolution of our generation is the discovery that human beings, by changing the inner attitudes of their minds, can change the outer aspects of their lives." However, changing the inner attitudes of one's mind takes much more than a momentary shift of thinking—it requires focus. When the mind's energy is consistently focused on a particular aim and backed up with persistence and hard work, it can and will accomplish seemingly miraculous things.

> When the mind's energy is consistently focused on a particular aim and backed up with persistence and hard work, it can and will accomplish seemingly miraculous things.

If people try to achieve success by dangling their toes in six or eight ventures instead of ever diving into one

112

that really matters and giving it their all, they are generally headed for a sad awakening. Split focus will hurt a leader's success.

On the other hand, consciously directed focus can be a very powerful tool to achieving success. John Assaraf shared a story of his own powerful experience with this principle:[25]

In his early years of learning the principle of visualization and focus, he made a dream board and posted pictures of all sorts of things to represent how he wanted his future life to look.

Years later, after lots of hard work, he found himself unpacking boxes in his brand-new house. As he unpacked, he came upon a box that held his early dream board. He couldn't believe what he saw.

In the section dedicated to his future home, he saw a photograph he had cut out of an old landscaping magazine. At the time he'd made the dream board, he hadn't known where the house was located or how much it would cost—just that it was pretty and that he'd like to have one like it someday.

He looked at the picture and almost wept. It was *his* house—the same house he had just bought and renovated. This experience can be a huge inspiration to mentors and mentees who really understand it. However, it's crucial that they recognize the next step in the process. People who find success through the power of focus do so because they recognize that it isn't a quick fix. It's an excellent tool—a tool designed to help people concentrate and optimize their tenacity.

Mentors and protégés who think they can get away without working hard will likely meet with significant disappointment in life and limited success. Vision and hard work are both needed.

WORKSHOP

Create a dream board to help you visualize and focus on your dreams.

Get a piece of cardstock, tape off a section of your wall, or set aside any flat surface where you can post pictures to represent the various aspects of the life you really want to be living, for example:

- Your dream house
- Your dream family life and relationships
- Your dream self
- The adventures you want to explore
- The successes you want to achieve
- The impact you want to have on the world
- Charities or causes you want to support

Once you have your surface ready, find images in magazines or online to represent each of the pieces of your dream life, and attach them to the surface. This is your dream board.

Now, for it to work, you should spend a few minutes every day looking at your vision board and telling your mind what you want from it.

Along with this visualization, your success will require a lot of hard work and tenacity. Focus will help you center in on your dream, but you'll still have to work hard to achieve it.

As you work, trust the process. Success doesn't immediately show up on your doorstep just because you make a fancy montage of photos on the wall; it takes time and effort. But the montage can help. As you consistently visualize, focus, work hard, and fight for what you want, results will start to come, and you will find successes—and probably some failures. Keep your focus firm and continue pushing forward.

You should also remember to trust God throughout this process. He knows what He's doing. Sometimes we don't get things the way we wanted or expected them, but God always has a design for us.

Sometimes we do find the exact results we'd hoped for, but often we find something even better than we could have imagined. And occasionally we find nothing but a long list of enormously valuable lessons and a new God-given vision of what we need to do next. But when we truly trust God, and genuinely work our hardest, He doesn't leave us hanging.

Share this exercise with your mentees, so they too can take advantage of the power of focus.

33

STARVE THE PROBLEM; FEED THE OPPORTUNITY

Peter Drucker said, "Effective people are not problem minded; they're opportunity minded. They feed opportunities and starve problems." Mentors should pay close attention to what both they and their mentees are focusing on.

Since the power of focus is so potent, it's especially important to focus on positive things. Whatever a person dedicates focus and energy to will likely continue in her life, so it's dangerous to focus on weaknesses, failures, or problems. This concept is a mixture of harnessing the power of focus and turning failures into opportunities.

Helen Keller expressed it beautifully when she said, "When one door of happiness closes, another opens, but often we look so long at the closed door that we do not see the one that has been opened for us."[26]

Helen Keller's life is a great illustration of this idea. Imagine if she had spent her whole life focusing on the negative. She certainly could have found problems to feed, which would have starved the opportunities that existed all around her. Fortunately, she had a great mentor, who helped her get past the victim mentality of overfed problems and see a world of opportunity.

Keller was able to be a great success in life and an inspiration to many others because she focused her energy on the positive. When she found closed doors, she moved on and searched for new ones that were opened to her.

If people focus on closed doors, not only will they miss the newly opened ones, they will also likely see more closed doors than others see. We tend to find what we're looking for, and those who look for problems usually find them.

In a way, people who believe that the whole world is against them are absolutely right. If they focus on their problems, their efforts will be begging those problems to grow and increase.

A mentor who has this negative outlook on life will usually

> **If people focus on closed doors, not only will they miss the newly opened ones, they will also likely see more closed doors than others see.**

be more of a pain to his mentees than a blessing. A mentee with this mentality is fortunate if he has a great mentor to help him starve the problem and feed the opportunity. Orrin Woodward said, "If you fill your head with positive thoughts, there won't be any room left for negative ones." Mentors should focus on the positive and thus attract more of it—and teach their mentees to do the same.

34

MENTORS AS TALENT SCOUTS

A mentor who understands the powers of decline that are at work in the world knows that she must become a talent scout to maximize her impact as a leader.

Everyone has the potential to become a genius, but because of the laws of decline, few people are willing to pay the price to really tap into that genius. Recognizing this sad fact, mentors should be careful to target their effort to those who will actually do something with it.

The story of the young man who had read the mentor's book—and his friend who hadn't—illustrates this point very well. A mentor who spreads her focus between twelve protégés, when only two of them are actually embracing the task of becoming a tenacious leader-in-training, is actually being less effective than she could be if she put her focus toward just the two who were both ready to work and worth her time. (Of course, she needs to mentor a number of people to find the two protégés.)

> **Everyone has the potential to become a genius, but because of the laws of decline, few people are willing to pay the price to really tap into that genius.**

As the saying goes, "A bird in the hand is worth two in the bush." Three mentees who are fighting for their dreams are better than ten who are flitting around hoping to find an easy road. Good mentors must learn to recognize the right kind of mentee—one who is really willing to walk the rocky, uphill path to success. In other words, good mentors must become "Tenacity Scouts."

One mentor shared the following story:

I'm often approached by people who want me to mentor them, but I've learned that my time is precious, so I don't waste it on people who won't really value it as they should.

Once, a young woman came up to me at a book signing I did in her neighborhood. She wanted me to be her personal mentor. I immediately said no, as was my practice, but told her I could recommend some good books. She took the sticky note with three or four titles on it and she walked away, looking a bit dejected. I thought that was the end of it.

A few months later, my assistant told me there was a girl from Arizona on the phone for me. Could I take the call?

It took me a few minutes to recall who this girl was, but when I realized it was the girl from the book signing, I was shocked.

She told me she had read the titles I had given her, plus the biographies of two of the authors, and she had some questions for me. She asked if I had an hour or two to discuss the books with her. I had a busy schedule that day, so I had to decline, but we scheduled a call for the next evening.

When we discussed the books, I discovered that she really had read them all—quite thoroughly. There were some things she didn't understand, and even a few we disagreed on, but it was an interesting conversation, to say the least.

When we finished discussing the books, she had just one more question for me: Wouldn't I please reconsider and agree to be her mentor?

When I saw how hard she would work, not only to pursue her own success by reading great books, but also by persistently seeking out the mentor she wanted, despite obvious obstacles, I knew she was going to be successful someday, and I wanted to help get her there.

Long story short, I said yes, and over the years I've found her to be one of my most dedicated and successful mentees and associates.

Mentors should remember to focus their time and energy on those mentees who are really willing to take advantage of it. This means learning to recognize the signs of real tenacity.

> **Mentors should look for diligence, tenacity, ingenuity, initiative, optimism, and vision in prospective mentees.**

If a mentee is easily deterred from achieving what she wants on the small things—such as reading a book, doing the basic work of success, or seeking out a good mentor—she is very unlikely to stick to her dreams when the real challenges come. Mentors should look for diligence, tenacity, ingenuity, initiative, optimism, and vision in prospective mentees. If mentees don't have these qualities, they probably won't choose to be in the 10 percent who really matter, and that 10 percent is where great mentors should put the power of their focus. Of course, the best way to find out if a person has the right traits is to give her a chance—put her to work!

35

MORE LEADERS = MORE RESULTS

Good mentors know that better results will come through the efforts of more leaders. This is why it's so important for them to be selective in their choice of mentees. They know that to make the biggest difference in the world, they need to raise the highest possible number of leader–mentors.

Mentors who build mentors who build mentors will accomplish huge dreams and change the world. This is why they have to be Tenacity Scouts. They can't afford to waste their time putting energy into dead-end lines that

121

just use it up and never put anything out; they have to put it where it will flow and grow.

American baseball player Jackie Robinson said, "Life is not important except in the impact it has on other lives."[27] This is especially true when it comes to mentoring. If a mentor's efforts do not impact the lives of his mentees—and in such a way that they impact the lives of many others—they really aren't worth much. Mentoring is all about impact.

Mark Twain said, "The man who does not read has no advantage over the man who cannot read." The ability to read, think, act, mentor, or change the world is not a good in and of itself. It is not the mentor's ability to accomplish amazing things that sets him apart as great; it is what he chooses to do with that ability.

Just as thinking isn't worth much without action, and action isn't worth much without positive results, mentoring isn't worth much unless it leads to change and success. The effect of a mentor's abilities gives them their meaning.

A man of great wisdom will not be called a great mentor unless he shares it, using it to help shape other great minds and mentors.

The goal of great mentors should be to achieve great results. The more capable people there are working toward something, the more likely they are to achieve their goals. There is power in numbers. Imagine all those well-trained minds focusing their energy into one big dream and then tenaciously climbing toward it, bringing others to the cause all the time. This is a powerful team of 10 percenters.

Great mentors should see the big picture. Mentoring, just like every other action, is about results. The more great mentors in the playing field, the stronger their impact will be.

Mentors mentor for impact.

36

USING THE SOCRATIC METHOD

Socrates is one of the most famous mentors in history, and we can learn from his example. He taught by asking questions and allowing his mentees to answer. His lessons consisted of a directed string of questions that led the mentee from one state of thinking to another.

This method was particularly powerful because by targeting his questions based on their answers, Socrates ensured that his mentees followed every step of the dialogue. The mentees were required to learn how to think by coming head to head with their mentor in a philosophical discussion based on questioning and answering.

Learning in this way is especially effective for a mentor whose goal is to build and shape other great mentors and leaders because it pushes the mentee to become an independent thinker.

In many educational methods, questions are asked by the student, and the teacher gives the answer, which is always "right." The Socratic method, however, does the reverse. The mentor asks a question, and the mentee has to think of an answer and then be able to support it against the continuing questions of the mentor.

> **Mentors should frequently let the mentee do most of the talking and come up with his own answers, gently guiding him through the process rather than taking it over.**

For the same reason that inspiring is more powerful than requiring, this method is very effective.

When a mentee is able to understand why two and two make four, he knows much more than if he has merely memorized the equation 2+2=4. Just the same, a mentee who has to think through a question and decide what he believes is more equipped to be a mentor and a leader than one who was merely told all the answers and assured they were true.

Of course, having the direction of a wise and experienced mentor throughout this process is very helpful because it intensifies the likelihood of correct assumptions and conclusions. But mentors should frequently let the mentee do most of the talking and come up with his own answers, gently guiding him through the process rather than taking it over.

An interesting literary example of this is the way that Elizabeth Bennet questions Mr. Darcy in Jane Austen's *Pride and Prejudice*. At nearly every encounter, she asks him a deep question that forces him to look into himself and find a response. As soon as he responds, she proceeds to ask a question about his answer, and so on. As irritating and intoxicating as this proves to be for Darcy, it really forces him to think and to defend his opinions.

She continues the process until he is either driven to admit he is wrong and change himself or is made strong in his conviction. She rarely lectures him on how he ought to change but encourages him to come to the realization on his own. Though she isn't a formal mentor, she is a great mentor to him, and her Socratic style helps him overcome many weaknesses and misconceptions.

The Socratic method can be a great way to build protégés who really know *how* to think rather than just *what* to think, and knowing how to think is essential to solid mentoring and leadership.

> **In business mentoring, the Socratic approach is one of the best ways to help people really think—and change.**

Of course, there is a place for mentors to teach mentees what to think (hopefully, in early parenting), but this generally consists of the establishment of a moral code and the like. Even this will benefit from a Socratic journey when the mentee has reached a suitable level of maturity and intellectual capacity.

In business mentoring, the Socratic approach is one of the best ways to help people really think—and change.

37

WHY MENTORS ARE LISTENERS

Great mentors must be listeners in at least three ways.

The first is in getting to know their mentees. Orrin Woodward and Chris Brady wrote, "The key for a mentor is to listen. A mentor must learn to draw people out, to get them talking about themselves and their past experiences in ways that perhaps they rarely do. If the mentor gets someone talking long enough, he can learn nearly everything there is to know about him or her. It is as if the mentor is saying, 'I want to get to know who you are so I can help you accomplish your dreams.'"

Mentors should listen with this mentality in all their conversations with their mentees—not just at the beginning of the relationship. Mentees should always feel loved and heard when speaking to their mentor.

The second way of listening is in teaching. As a mentor teaches, using the Socratic method or any other teaching style, he should be listening for his mentee's thought patterns. If he listens well, he will learn a lot about how his mentee is progressing and what she needs now. If a mentor isn't listening to the natural progress reports that come from casual conversation, he shouldn't expect to be able to effectively direct the next steps of his mentee.

For example, a certain mentor called a few of his mentees together to discuss an article he had found and enjoyed. As the conversation progressed, he noticed that one woman in the group kept getting frustrated because she thought the others were interpreting the text too abstractly.

"I don't even know where you're getting that! It doesn't say that *anywhere* in that paragraph. Or in any other, for that matter," she said with a snort.

"I know the words don't explicitly say so, but I think the message definitely implies it—no question," replied another person in the group.

The woman rolled her eyes, but remained silent. It was not the first time this happened.

After the discussion, he called the woman into his office to discuss her progress.

"Would you like to know what I learned today, Rosa?" he asked after they had taken their seats.

"Okay," she said, smiling. She always got over her frustration quickly.

"I think you need to study this book," he handed her a volume off his shelf, "and bring me an outline of what you think the author's philosophy is. Sound good?"

"Sure." She noticed the author's name. "This is the same guy we discussed today, right?"

"Yeah. I think it will help you to understand what you read a bit better. That'll be fun, right?"

127

"No doubt," she said, half sarcastically.

"Don't worry; judging from our conversation earlier, I think you'll find it—interesting."

After she left, he opened the notebook he'd been writing in during the group discussion. He flipped to the page with her name on it and crossed off the first item on his list.

Rosa —

1. ~~needs to meet with me in person and receive an extra assignment.~~

2. needs to learn to do background study to increase her understanding of what she's reading.

3. needs an opportunity to teach this book to someone.

4. needs some good praise in the next few weeks— try to catch her doing something right.

5. needs a check-up call on Friday.

When he finished with Rosa's sheet, he continued on to his other lists.

Because this mentor listened carefully during the discussion, he was able to assess both the progress and needs of his mentees and give them the meaningful attention each one needed.

The third type of listening a great mentor needs to master is listening to and for valuable counsel from his own mentors. Mentors should realize that they don't know everything; there's always more to learn. As Brady and

Woodward said it, "Seeking counsel from qualified sources is one of the most effective ways for a leader to learn."

Effective mentors are generally themselves tenacious protégés. They should have all sorts of mentors—formal mentors, hero-mentors, books, and media—and they should be willing to learn from the wisdom of their own mentees and treat it as what it is—real mentoring.

> **Effective mentors are generally themselves tenacious protégés. They should have all sorts of mentors— formal mentors, hero-mentors, books, and media—and they should be willing to learn from the wisdom of their own mentees.**

Plutarch said, "Know how to listen, and you will profit even from those who talk badly." Truth is everywhere. A mentor who learns how to listen will learn all sorts of great things from a variety of sources.

Learning to listen in all these ways will increase the success of mentors and help them guide their mentees to success as well.

38

How to Listen

Mentors should listen with empathy. When it's time to listen, a mentor should focus on *hearing* and *understanding* her mentee—not just trying to fix him or his problems.

Stephen Covey explained that one of the main obstacles to empathetic listening is that people don't listen to understand; they listen to respond. "They're filtering everything through their own paradigm, reading their autobiography into other people's lives....They're constantly projecting their own home movies onto other people's behavior. They prescribe their own glasses for everyone with whom they interact."[28]

It is especially important that mentors learn how to listen in such a way that they actually understand their mentees. A mentor's wisdom and experience can be really helpful to a mentee facing a roadblock, but the mentor must really grasp where the mentee is coming from and how she is feeling before he goes off spouting prescriptions for an undiagnosed problem.

> One of the main obstacles to empathetic listening is that people don't listen to understand; they listen to respond.

In his book *The 7 Habits of Highly Effective People*, Covey shared the story of a father who came to him for help, saying, "I can't understand my kid. He just won't listen to me at all." Covey was surprised to hear this, but he tried to work with the man patiently.

He spent several minutes trying to lead the man to realize the weight of what he was saying, but in the end, he had to remind the man that generally when you're trying to understand a person, you should probably start by listening to what *he* says, not by making him listen to you. If this father was having difficulty understanding his son, it most likely wasn't just because his *son* wasn't listening.

Mentors should learn that while there is a time for sharing advice and offering solutions, that time usually comes after real understanding. The key is to listen to the mentee's words and also to listen to more than just the words. Mentors should learn to recognize whether their mentees are speaking in *sympathize* mode or *fix-it* mode.

When mentees are speaking in sympathize mode, mentors should listen with empathy and love; this isn't solution time, it's listen time. This is an opportunity to make the mentee feel that he is important, that what he has to say really matters to his mentor. He usually just wants to feel he isn't alone with his problems.

When the mentee is speaking in fix-it mode, he is ready to take the problem by the horns and find answers. At this point, he will often ask for advice, and it is appropriate for the mentor to talk solutions.

A mentor who takes the time and energy to understand his mentee's perspective will be able to correctly diagnose problems and needs before he starts spouting solutions. Often, as mentioned, a mentee just needs to be heard. When a mentor responds too quickly with solutions and quick fixes, it can make the mentee feel cut off and ignored rather than understood. Mentors should avoid the urge to supply answers before the mentee has had the opportunity to feel affirmed.

Empathetic listening builds trust to the point that the mentee is willing to accept and implement viable solutions when they do come. Listening with patience and understanding will not only help the mentor properly target areas of weakness; it will help set the tone for the hard work needed to strengthen those areas.

39

MENTORING STRENGTHS

In a 2011 article in *Harvard Business Review*, author Bill Barnett listed the following five steps to recognizing personal strengths:

1.   List your strengths.
2.   Ask others for input.
3.   Revisit past feedback.

4. "Hire" yourself.
5. Revisit your strengths list.[29]

Mentors should consider adapting this exercise for their mentees.

Make a list of what you perceive your mentee's strengths to be: What knowledge and abilities has he developed through past business experience and education? What natural talents, gifts, and tendencies does she have? What does he do best? What does she *like* to do best? What are his passions and interests?

> **Recognizing strengths can help mentors and mentees find the right direction for significant progress.**

Ask your mentee what he thinks his main strengths are. He will often come up with a few you hadn't thought of or spark new ideas for you to add to your list.

Look back to previous praisings, course corrections, and meetings. What strengths did you observe?

"Hire" him. Pretend you're interviewing him for a position in your company today. (If he works for you already, hire him for *his* job, as though he didn't have it yet.) Look at everything you know about him—strengths, weaknesses, performance. Would he get the job, or wouldn't he? What would swing the scale one way or the other?

Go back to the original list and make additions and changes as needed.

Mentors should also give their mentees a copy of this exercise. When both mentor and mentee have completed it, they should set up a special meeting to discuss and consider what they learned.

Recognizing strengths can help mentors and mentees find the right direction for significant progress. Assessing strengths allows mentors to both build on strengths and strengthen weaknesses.

Possibly the best way to build on strengths is to find frequent occasion to use them. Mentors should look for opportunities to push their mentees to exhibit their strengths. As mentees push the limits of their strengths, they are forced to grow. It's a lot like building muscles: push them to their limits, stretch them, and in the rest-and-recovery phase, they build themselves up bigger and stronger.

When a mentee is pushed to the edges of his strength, he learns new things about himself and finds new ways to be better. Then, in his rest-and-recovery time, he is able to implement what he learned about the limits of his strength and build himself up bigger and stronger.

Eleanor Roosevelt said, "You gain strength, courage, and confidence by every experience in which you really stop to look fear in the face. You are able to say to yourself, 'I have lived through this horror. I can take the next thing that comes along.'...You must do the thing you think you cannot do."[30]

In strength-building, mentors should first assess strengths and then provide opportunities for the mentee to stretch them further. Assessing strengths first not only shows the mentor what to work on but also gives him a sense of how much the mentee can handle in being pushed to build those strengths. Mentors should be careful not to push mentees beyond what they can take.

Even where real talent and strength exist, tenacity is required to unlock the greatest levels of success. Napoleon Hill said, "Strength and growth come only through continuous effort and struggle." Mentors should help their mentees understand that to be truly fruitful, they must work hard to build their strengths as well as overcome their weaknesses.

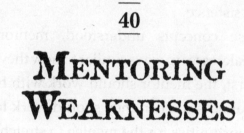

40

MENTORING WEAKNESSES

Effectively mentoring weaknesses is a matter of appropriately combining the techniques of effective reprimands, tenacity trumping talent, mentoring strengths, and tact.

When dealing with weaknesses, a mentor should make his love for the mentee abundantly clear. Weakness-strengthening should be done with aggressive love and humble truth. There should be a well-established environment of trust and closeness *before* the mentor starts digging into weaknesses.

Mentees who have been effectively taught the power of tenacity will find it easier to accept their weaknesses at face value and then beat them. Changing weakness into strength is something that takes a lot of work, but it can be done. Mentors and mentees should understand that overcoming weakness is a matter of determinedly fighting for personal improvement and it is absolutely worth the effort. Hard work can transform a weakness into a strength. Mentors should constantly remind their mentees about the power of persistence.

> **The process of changing weakness to strength should be taken step by step and customized to the strengths and vulnerabilities of the individual mentee.**

With these concepts understood, mentors should approach weaknesses in ways similar to how they approach strengths. First, the mentor should work with his mentee to assess weaknesses. Then they should work together to find safe opportunities for the mentee to stretch herself in order to obtain growth and improvement.

Throughout the process, mentors should be careful not to move too quickly; nobody needs to be burned with truth coffee. The process of changing weakness to strength should be taken step by step and customized to the strengths and vulnerabilities of the individual mentee.

Tom Peters said that "a passive approach to professional growth will leave you by the wayside." This is true of any type of growth. To grow and overcome weakness, a person must actively employ smart action. Mentors should lovingly and tactfully help their mentees understand and act upon this principle in every aspect of their lives (but only one at a time).

41

WHEN TO EMPHASIZE STRENGTHS OVER WEAKNESSES

Building strengths and overcoming weaknesses are vital aspects of being a good leader. As mentioned earlier, a good mentor should know how to help her mentees accomplish this. An important part of doing this, however, is knowing *when* to emphasize which one.

While there is power in the act of sitting down, looking at weaknesses, and brainstorming ways to overcome them, overemphasizing weaknesses will feed the problem and thus starve the opportunities for the individual to actually progress. Mentors should take care in their timing and emphasis to be certain they don't put too much focus on potentially negative things. Emphasizing weaknesses to the right degree and at the right times can be a positive and exciting thing, but overemphasis can lead to a damaging mind-set.

In fact, the best way to overcome weaknesses is simply to put the focus and emphasis on building and developing strengths instead. Marilyn vos Savant said, "Success is achieved by developing our strengths, not by eliminating our weaknesses." Mentees who emphasize developing strengths rather than fixing weaknesses usually accomplish more of both.

There is, however, an important time for mentors to emphasize certain types of weakness. Mentors *must* directly address weaknesses when those weaknesses are preventing the protégé's strengths from really working for his benefit.

In *Launching a Leadership Revolution*, Chris Brady and Orrin Woodward explained that sometimes when leaders have weaknesses that are so glaring as to be ranked at zero percent effectiveness, those weaknesses actually get in the way of certain strengths. Likewise, 1 percent effectiveness in one area will bring down the effectiveness of any leader.

Mentors should help their protégés be honest with themselves about their strengths and weaknesses so they can improve their overall effectiveness and influence.

> **Mentors *must* directly address weaknesses when those weaknesses are preventing the protégé's strengths from really working for his benefit.**

Brady and Woodward continued, "We don't control where we start our journeys, but we *do* control what we do once we've started. The goal is to take what we've been given and do the most we can with it."[31]

Mentors or mentees may have significant weaknesses, but that doesn't mean they are hopeless cases. The important thing is to recognize real weakness and work to improve it, while also recognizing real strengths, so they aren't lost or confused for weakness.

Daniel J. Boorstin said, "We suffer primarily not from our vices or our weaknesses, but from our illusions. We are haunted, not by reality, but by those images we have put in their place." Sometimes, when a mentee believes he has certain weaknesses, he will refuse to work in certain areas because he's already decided they're too far above him. This mentality is extremely limiting, and mentors should do their best to help a mentee avoid it.

Sometimes mentors need to emphasize "weaknesses" because they are, in fact, nothing but false beliefs. Even in these cases, mentors should emphasize building strengths with the mentee, though their specific intent may be to help the mentee reframe certain false beliefs and perceived weaknesses.

Mentors can do this by taking a few important steps.

First, be sure to give sufficient praise. Praising a mentee's real strengths and accomplishments can go a long way toward helping him throw out false perceptions. If his mentor consistently tells him that something's a strength, it's harder for him to keep believing that it's a weakness.

Second, offer genuine recognition. Mentors should go a step further—when it's appropriate—and give the mentee recognition by offering him extra opportunities to shine

139

in those areas and following up with heartfelt and meaningful praise.

Third, consider doing an exercise with the mentee to properly evaluate her strengths and weaknesses. If she understands that her mentor sees these things as strengths, her confidence and trust will usually increase.

By doing these three things to reframe false perceptions, mentors can help mentees have truer and healthier perceptions of both their real strengths and their real weaknesses.

As mentors focus on building strengths and help their mentees recognize actual needs, they will be setting the tone for powerful growth and improvement.

42

MENTORING QUESTIONS

Great mentors are different from professors, teachers, or researchers who lecture, instruct, or investigate and publish. Mentors cover a lot more ground than the others. They give assignments and follow up, they coach, they tutor, and they give important personal help and guidance. But in reality, this is not the basis of mentoring. The very basis of mentoring is asking questions.

We have already discussed many important questions for mentors to ask themselves—both in self-searching and in considering mentees—but these next seven questions are central to effective mentoring:

1. What are my biggest dreams?

2. What are my biggest fears?

3. What is my biggest source or object of anger?

4. What three things do I most need from my mentor in the next few months?

5. What three things do I need my mentor to be?

6. If some scientific discovery gave me an extra hour in each day, what would I do with that hour?

7. Based on my answers to questions one through six, what one thing do I want to change in my life?[32]

Knowing these answers and making the change will help mentors and mentees to continuously live a purposeful life and to achieve their dreams.

> **The very basis of mentoring is asking questions.**

WORKSHOP[33]

On a blank piece of paper, make three columns. Column one should be labeled "Questions," column two should be labeled "Me," and column three should be labeled, "Insert mentee's name."

Once you have your page and columns ready, it's time to start asking yourself the seven questions.

1.   What are my biggest dreams?
      - What are my top five biggest dreams?
      - What are my most important dreams?
      - What do I dream of doing or being?
      - What do I really want most?

Write these questions in column one and then answer them for yourself in column two.

When this is done, spend some time thinking about your dreams:

      - Why do they matter to me?
      - Who would I be without them?
      - How important are they?
      - Are they central to my life?
      - Are they a lot of fun?

When you've finished, write answers in column three as if your mentee were answering the questions. (For example, *Gina's top five biggest dreams are....*)

2.   What are my biggest fears?

Answer for yourself in column two and for your mentee in column three.

3. What is my biggest source or object of anger?

Answer, following the same pattern as before.

As a mentor, facing your fears and anger is essential. Even if you never share the conversation with anyone, doing these exercises can help your ability to mentor, lead, empathize, care for, and understand the people you work with.

4. What three things do I most need from my mentor in the next few months?

Answer for yourself, then for your mentee (e.g., *What three things does Gina need from me in the next few months?*).

5. What three things do I need my mentor to be?

Note the significant difference between *doing* and *being*. Mentees are influenced by both.

6. If some scientific discovery gave me an extra hour in each day, what would I do with it?

Use column two to answer this for yourself. In column three of this question, write what you would recommend for your mentee to do with the extra hour.

7.   Based on my answers to questions one through six, what one thing do I want to change in my life?

Write either the one thing that would make the most positive difference in your life if you changed it right now or the one thing you really think you *should* change. Then make a plan to implement it, and get to work!

Once you've done this, do the same for your mentee, and recommend the number-one change you came up with. Remember, you can't compel change, but explain how you think this would improve her life.

Many of your protégés would benefit from going through this exercise themselves, so when you find one you think is ready, pass a copy along, and be ready to offer help as needed.

43

CREATING THE ENVIRONMENT FOR SUCCESS

In showing a good example of constant self-improvement and hard work, mentors are already taking the necessary steps toward creating the environment for success.

When a mentor is committed to the path of success, the environment is close to captured. However, there are two important steps that he can follow up with to make up the difference.

The first important step is setting the right kind of huge and important goals. These goals should be such that they can inspire passion in those who come in contact with them. Just as in writing, the most important element is having a big, deep idea, the most important element of success in leadership is having a cause that really, deeply matters.

In writing, you may have perfect language, grammar, and style, but if you have nothing to say, the writing can *TRUE, THIS! & WHERE I'M AT.* never be really great and probably won't amount to much. In an organization, you may have the perfect model, execution, and talent, but if there isn't an important product, cause, or purpose, it can never achieve true greatness.

> Once mentors and mentees have established a concrete and worthy goal, the second step to creating the environment for success is making that goal totally achievable.

This same principle applies to mentoring. A mentor may have all the right experience and background and a mentee who is perfectly ready to be helped, but unless they have an important and meaningful goal for their interaction, their relationship can never really accomplish anything. Success needs definition. Dream big!

Once mentors and mentees have established a concrete and worthy goal, the second step to creating the environment for success is making that goal totally achievable. Mentors should help mentees find bite-sized chunks of the goal to chew on one at a time. This way they not only have a clear end in mind; they have the tools they need to start walking toward it.

Success needs to be possible. Get to work!

And of course, as mentors in this kind of environment provide the example of how it's all possible, they will add to the driving force that takes mentees and turns them into shining new successes. Example, as was discussed in an earlier chapter, is one of the most powerful motivators. Especially when added to these other elements, a good example will help mentees work hard even when it's tough, believe in the possibility of the dream, and pick themselves up when they stumble.

Success needs an example. Show them how!

An environment where there is a clear understanding of what success means, an available avenue for achieving that success, and a few shining examples of people who are willing to put in the effort necessary to get there is an environment of success.

Of course, even if the environment of success exists, that doesn't mean that anyone who unwittingly stumbles into it will suddenly find herself a master of success. Naturally, each person will still have to work hard and face obstacles before she reaches her dreams. But what an environment of success *will* do is help provide people with the tools and support they will need to become successful, should they choose to use them.

Mentors who create an environment of success with their mentees will find it to be one of the most powerful tools of leadership.

44

HOW TO LEAD A GROUP DISCUSSION

One great tool for mentors to consider is the use of group discussions. This means the mentor calls several mentees together to converse about a shared experience in a debrief-style discussion. This could mean a book they all read, a seminar they all attended, a world event they're all familiar with, and so forth.

Group discussion is one of the best ways for mentees to solidify opinions and interpret experiences in meaningful and practical ways. If these discussions don't have the proper guidance, however, they can often get quite heated and end in unnecessary conflict. For this reason, it is important that a well-informed mentor bring his wisdom to the table in

> **The key to leading a group discussion is running it with the right balance of speaking, asking, and listening.**

such discussions. Mentors should know how to properly referee group discussions to avoid contention while steering toward the most meaningful lessons and approach to a given topic.

Mentors who learn when to lecture, when to ask questions, and when to remain silent will find group discussion to be an extremely beneficial exercise for their mentees.

Mentors should look at group discussion as an opportunity to learn from their mentees, as well as about them. By drawing mentees out to discuss things they're working on and learning, a mentor can learn about their strengths and weaknesses as well as their needs and a new strategic direction of focus for their future development.

The key to leading a group discussion is running it with the right balance of speaking, asking, and listening. A speech from the mentor can have a powerful effect on mentees, but this is not a group discussion.

Here are two great ways for a mentor to begin a group discussion:

1. The mentor shares his thoughts about the shared experience, teaches his mentees some of the most important things he got from it for two to four minutes, and then opens it up for them to do the same. After his introduction, he should remember to listen for a while, not just take the whole time speaking his own mind. People will generally learn more when they have the opportunity to think about things and

present their own ideas than when they hear a long recital of someone else's views.

2. The mentor asks a profound question for the mentees to discuss. (This should be a thoroughly thought-out question, not just something random.) Once her question is asked, the mentor should wait for the mentees to search for their own answers. This allows mentees to consider the topic from many angles and with a deep and important direction.

Of course, these are only two ways to begin to get ideas flowing; there are many others.

It is valuable for the mentor to lightly pepper the discussion with well-timed questions. This keeps it on track and protects against unhelpful tangents. It also ensures that the mentees will have time to talk about the ideas involved that really matter most, rather than "never getting to them."

Mentors should also spend a fair amount of time allowing others to talk. This gives mentees the chance to experience important leadership and speaking opportunities. Good mentors know that real leadership often requires the ability to effectively speak in front of others and communicate points and ideas in public

> One of the things that makes good mentoring so important is that it facilitates the transfer of wisdom from those who have it to those who seek it.

settings. Group discussions can be a great place for mentees to develop and practice those skills.

And of course, mentors should be willing and ready to share their own ideas and wisdom when the situation requires it. One of the things that makes good mentoring so important is that it facilitates the transfer of wisdom from those who have it to those who seek it. The important thing is for the mentor to know when to share her wisdom outright and when to share it by holding her tongue.

Asking a protégé to lead a group discussion can also be a great tool for mentors, as it gives the protégé much-needed leadership experience while allowing the mentor to watch and evaluate his performance.

45

OPTIMIZING STRENGTHS IN TEAMS

Good mentors know that a leader has strengths in various areas. They also know that different leaders have different strengths in complementary areas. Part of mentoring, especially in a business setting, is knowing how to set up teams in such a way that they achieve the highest level of success.

It's interesting that the world often thinks of leadership as one guy directing and running a bunch of people unworthy to lead and mentoring as one guy magnani-mously sharing his genius and sagacity with his inferiors. In reality, both leadership and mentoring are absolutely team sports.

Brian Tracy said, "Teamwork is so important that it is virtually impossible for you to reach the heights of your capabilities or make the money that you want without becoming very good at it."

Mentors and leaders who want to find true success and make a tangible difference in the world should learn to team up with those who share their dreams and can add new strengths to the mix. A group of five strong leaders who share the same strengths and dreams will, with hard work, become hugely successful. But five leaders with a shared dream and a variety of strengths can be even more successful. The same is true of mentors.

A protégé can benefit immensely from having a mentor with the foresight, vision, and humility to help him find several other mentors. Mentors should encourage their mentees to seek out mentoring and counsel from other worthy sources and even recommend those they feel are particularly suited to the personality and needs of the individual mentee in question.

A fantastic example of this is the Marvel story of the Avengers (The Incredible Hulk, Iron Man, Black Widow, Hawkeye, Captain America, Thor, and others). They are all great leaders with their own brand of success. Each is effective on his or her own, but when they come together and form a team, combining their strengths amplifies their power to new levels. They accomplish much more as a team than they ever could have as individuals.

Mentors and mentees will find a higher rate of success if they join effort with the right teams. Mentors should team up with other great mentors who have complementing strengths in order to optimize their impact and effectiveness. And they should arrange the relationships of their various mentees in such a way that they have the greatest opportunity to do the same.

46

How to Mentor for Good Public Speaking

Leaders often find that being good at public speaking is necessary to further their success. A person can have a leadership mentality and remain alone for a short time, but it will not last. For leadership to really soar, it has to involve more than one person. More often than not, this calls for public speaking, and the ability to effectively analyze and move an audience is one of the most valuable tools for a leader to have.

That said, mentors who want to build successful leaders should probably learn how to mentor for good public speaking.

As with any important leadership skill, a good portion of learning *how* to do it is actually doing it. Mentors who want their mentees to be good public speakers should give them lots of opportunities to practice public speaking. Personal experience and hard work may be the best ways to learn something, especially if that something is a new skill. There really isn't a way for mentors to download ability into their mentees' brains, but there is a way they can help them develop new abilities or strengthen those they already have. That way is action. Again, mentees who want to be good public speakers need to speak.

That said, there are a few things a mentor can do before, during, and after a mentee's speech that will help him optimize his experience:

1. **Remember the Power of Ideas**

    D. H. Lawrence said, "Be still when you have nothing to say; when genuine passion moves you, say what you've got to say, and say it hot."

    > **The most important element of any speech—and, indeed, of any speaker—is the idea behind it.**

    The really good public speakers in the world are very rarely people who have nothing to say. The most important element of any speech—and, indeed, of any speaker—is the idea behind it. The point of public speaking should not be merely to stand up and sound pretty.

Even poetry and comedy (both areas of public speaking that tend to focus a lot on the words themselves) should be about more than words put together in clever ways. The most effective poets and comedians know that the human soul reacts most powerfully to entertainment that also speaks powerful messages to the heart.

In short, mentors should teach their mentees that the first step to good public speaking is to have an important message to share. Everyone knows that it's easier to speak when you actually have something passionate to say.

Cicero, a famous Roman statesman and orator, said, "A good orator is pointed and impassioned." Passion and clarity are derived from ideas. When a speaker has an idea he is passionate about, he actually has a point.

2. **Watch and Learn**

One thing that can really help a mentee prepare to tackle the podium is watching and listening to other great speakers and learning from them. Mentors should encourage their mentees to consistently put themselves in an environment of good speaking. They should go to great speeches, listen to audio recordings of great speakers, and study the best historical and contemporary speeches and speakers.

As they do, they should be dissecting the information they gather. Mentors should teach their mentees to ask themselves the following questions after they watch, listen to, or read the work of any good speaker:

1. Was this a great speaker and/or speech?
2. What made this speaker great or not great?
3. How could he have been better?
4. In what ways should I emulate him?
5. What strengths and weaknesses do the speaker and I share? How can this help me improve my speaking?
6. How did he relate to the audience?
7. How did he convince people to care about his point?
8. How did he communicate his passion for his idea?
9. What did he leave me wanting to do?
10. Is there anything else I can learn from this experience?

Answering these questions will help mentees learn public speaking techniques along with all the other great ideas they glean from encountering great speakers and speeches. People can naturally learn lots of little skills from watching other people do things they want to master themselves. Consciously noting these lessons will make them even more powerful and easier to remember and implement.

3. **Critique and Constructive Criticism**

Dale Carnegie said, "There are always three speeches for every one you actually gave. The one you practiced, the one you gave, and the one you wish you gave." Almost everyone who ever gives a speech, whether good or bad, sits down to the ovation of the audience and outwardly braves the storm of inner commentary. As he walks to his chair, he bombards himself with a list of things he should have said better or differently or not at all.

A good mentor teaches her mentee to smile at the commentary and take notes. This is one of the most powerful aspects of public speaking that a mentor can teach her mentee. How many times has he sat for hours with writer's block, trying to come up with the right words to express his message? And now, all of the sudden, he is hit with a seemingly never-ending burst of inspiration!

Mentors should teach their mentees to take full advantage of the after-speech siege of beautiful phrases and powerful expression. Some of the best stuff a speaker comes up with often comes in a fit of post-speech self-critique.

It's important that mentors help their mentees see this self-critique in a positive light. If a mentee feels like a complete loser after every speech because he is too critical of himself, it will likely be more hurtful than constructive. The moments after a speech should be seen as inspiration time, not self-destruction time.

Mentors should also have their mentees dissect their speeches using the same questions they use to learn from the speeches they watch, listen to, or read. This can be especially helpful if the mentor also answers the questions and they come together to compare notes and discuss them positively.

Mentors should also try to set aside time to meet with their mentee after each speech and give him any other praise, critique, or commentary they feel will help the speaker's skills.

In critique and constructive criticism, it is important for mentors to be tactful and loving. The mentor should not attack the mentee with more than he can handle. Advice should be given in manageable chunks, determined by the mentee's own level of readiness. Mentors can be firm, but they should avoid being hurtful. This should be a time for building, not tearing down.

As mentors do these three things and shower their mentees with speaking opportunities, they are likely to see great improvements in their mentees' ability to move an audience and effectively express ideas that matter.

47

How to Mentor for *Great* Public Speaking

This chapter is called "How to Mentor *for* Great Public Speaking" instead of "How to Mentor Great Public Speaking" because it is not about methods. It's about lessons. It isn't going to explain what mentors can do to turn their good-public-speaker mentees into great ones. It's going to explain what great mentors need to teach their mentees so those mentees can do what they need to do to become great public speakers.

The main difference between a good public speaker and a great public speaker is her ability to read an audience and adapt her speech in real time to fit its needs.

Alexander Gregg said, "There are three things to aim at in public speaking: first, to get into your subject, then to get your subject into yourself, and lastly, to get your subject into the heart of your audience." This chapter is about the third aim.

Ultimately, the purpose of public speaking is to get a message into the audience. Mentors should teach their mentees that the greatest speakers are those who speak to their audience so that their audience absorbs their message. As a mentor discusses different speakers (as well as the mentee's own speeches) with her mentee, she should make this one point abundantly clear.

After ideas, the most important part of public speaking is really speaking to your audience. Speakers should know their audience and prepare their speeches accordingly. The very best speakers learn to *feel* their audience as they speak and are willing to throw out their prepared speech if that's what the audience needs.

> **The main difference between a good public speaker and a great public speaker is her ability to read an audience and adapt her speech in real time to fit its needs.**

The same speech does not work for every audience, and a great speaker must individualize his message to the group he's giving it to so that they will really understand it and feel it.

Great public speaking is a form of great mentoring. It requires the speaker to know the audience and love it deeply. It requires him to personalize his message to the needs and abilities of the audience. It requires him to be creative in his presentation so that he can build up the hearts of several—or many—people at once.

Mentors who understand this can help their protégés understand it also. Knowing that great public speaking is like mentoring—all about the mentee's growth and development—will change the mind-set of the speaker and allow him to see the big picture.

The ability to read an audience and recognize its needs from a podium is something that can only come through practice and experience, but having the conscious knowledge that this is the goal will help speakers work for it.

A person who wants to be a great speaker should work hard and do all the things that will make him a good speaker. And then he should continue to speak and work harder. And through all this, he should remember that to be a great speaker, he must learn to know his audience and speak to it and forget the rest.

Bruce Lee famously said, "Learn the rules, master the rules, break the rules." To be a master, one must know and understand the rules; he must master them. But the mark of a genuine master is that he knows how and when to effectively break the rules.

This doesn't mean people should feel free to make their own rules or that the rules are meaningless—only a master can break the rules correctly. It means that rules matter—not because they're rules, but because they're right. And, when someone has paid the price to master the rules, he is able to recognize when something else is even more right than the rules.

Mentors should teach their protégés this important key to great speaking.

48

MENTORING TEAMS

One of the best ways to effectively mentor in cases where there are multiple mentees is to set them up in a team. This can help mentees in a variety of ways, as well as free up the time of the mentor and spread the work around so everyone gets more out of the experience. We've already talked about teamwork, but mentoring teams is an even higher level.

Mentees who work closely with a team of other mentees (who share their vision and purpose) will often find that their work and time are more rewarding. Mentees can be hugely motivated by the hard work of their teammates. After all, nobody wants to feel like the lowest common denominator or the guy who lost his team the gold cup. Mentees can help each other stay on track and push each other to new heights of achievement and success.

Being in good teams also enables mentees to experience various leadership roles, preparing them for greater leadership responsibility in the future.

> **Mentees who work closely with a team of other mentees (who share their vision and purpose) will often find that their work and time are more rewarding.**

161

Vince Lombardi said, "Individual commitment to a group effort—that is what makes a team work, a company work, a society work, a civilization work." When individuals come together and fight as a unified group, they are able to accomplish much more than if they had been content to battle as individuals.

Having the right kind of teams in the equation means that mentors will be able to share the burdens and the learning experiences with all the men and women they work with. When this is done well, everyone gains more time and more experience. Learning happens at elevated levels for everyone involved.

Mentors of teams should remember to let other people do their part and take their share in the leadership; that's one of the main points of a team. Ronald Reagan said, "Surround yourself with the best people you can find, delegate authority, and don't interfere as long as the policy you've decided upon is being carried out." This helps people at every stage to grow in more significant ways.

While this is true, it is vital that mentors of teams remember that teams *are* made up of individuals. Mentors should know each mentee on a personal level, even though they are a part of a bigger team. As mentioned, when a mentor sets up teams of mentees he really knows, he is able to strategically place them where their strengths, weaknesses, and challenges will be the most meaningful. And as mentors get to know new members of their team, they will be able to help them find their best place in the team, so they can optimize their results.

A good mentor should help his team see his vision and jump on board. People on his team who have captured the vision and who have been put in a place where they can really begin to make a difference often find themselves to be the closest of friends. A team fighting for a cause tends to become a sort of close-knit family.

Orrin Woodward wrote, "The best compliment you can pay a leader is to praise his/her team."[34] Mentoring teams is one of the life works of a real leader. A mentor's team is a reflection of her dream and her tenacity combined. As her team succeeds, she is succeeding. As her team becomes a family, she sees her family changing the world in all the right ways.

Mentoring vision-driven teams is what mentors should be aiming for. When this type of mentoring succeeds, it creates generation after generation of leader–mentors. As a mentor comes to know and love individuals well enough that they can become a solid and effective team, he generally begins to see his own dreams becoming more and more real as well.

49

INTEGRITY

One reason being a part of a real team is so motivating and effective is that it offers a situation of tangible accountability. As individuals report to their team on what they did and did not do and review what they had promised to do, a high standard of accountability is often easier to maintain.

Interestingly, often problems with low accountability are due not so much to lack of willpower as to lack of commitment.

> **One of the most important pieces of wisdom a mentor can pass on to his mentees is that integrity to self is completely vital to success.**

No matter how many times a man tells himself that he's going to get serious about his health or his schedule or building his business, if he never actually commits and gets to work, his "seriousness" about it won't count for much. Often when a person sits down to "commit" herself to something she feels strongly about, she will refuse to be accountable by leaving herself a number of loopholes—enough that if she isn't in the mood tomorrow, she can easily get out of the commitment because she left it wide open.

One of the most important pieces of wisdom a mentor can pass on to his mentees is that integrity to self is completely vital to success. A person who cannot trust himself, or who refuses to ever make himself the important promises and keep them, will simply never put in the work it takes to become successful.

And as with many big and powerful principles, this one starts with the smallest things.

Imagine a woman who says as she's settling down for sleep, "Tomorrow, I will wake up at 5:00 and exercise because I need to have time to do that and talk to my daughter about that one thing before she heads out." She sets her alarm and then turns out the light.

The next morning she hears the buzzer. What will she do? This is a time for an important decision. Will she give in to the ever-calling power of the pillow-addict in her mind, or will she follow through with her intention?

This seems like a trivial thing, but it has the potential to influence her future in many ways. People who are faced with this type of decision and choose the wrong path often find that their ability to follow through with their larger decisions deteriorates at the slightest opposition.

People who develop a habit of following through on those little decisions that everybody makes each day are simultaneously developing a habit of successful living. If a person does what she really knows she needs to do when it's little and easy, she is much more likely to do so when things are really challenging.

Many people have a tendency to shoot up warning flares whenever they sense a self-commitment coming on. As soon as a person starts to say, "I'll meet with twenty clients this month," his brain starts shrieking out a hundred exceptions: "Unless I get sick," or "Unless a friend calls me and wants to catch lunch this weekend," and the list goes on.

It is not detrimental to success to have these things suggested at the start. It is, however, practically detrimental when any of these loopholes make it into the actual commitment a person makes to himself.

The problem comes when a person's final answer is "I *will* do this...unless something gets in the way or comes up." In life, something always gets in the way; something always comes up.

Sometimes when a person receives new information, it is appropriate for her to change her course of action based on it. But a person who really desires success in life cannot be filling his world with soft commitments or if-I-feel-like-its on the off chance that he could be wrong. Indecision is almost always worse than a wrong decision. A person can learn and grow from failures and wrong turns, but indecision leaves her stagnant.

> "Never surrender convictions for convenience."
> —Orrin Woodward

Men and women who consistently fail to do the easy little things they tell themselves they really must do will likely also consistently fail to achieve their dreams, self-respect, and happiness. As Orrin Woodward counseled, "Never surrender convictions for convenience." Note the word *never* in this sentence. It really does mean "not ever." Mentors and mentees who follow through on their decisions, big *and* small, will find far more success than those who decide that since they woke up five times in the night, it's okay for them to skip exercise or that talk with their child.

166

A mentor who can trust himself will be much more trustworthy to his mentees. And that's what this really boils down to: trust and integrity. If a mentor allows his relationship with himself to become one where no trust exists, his relationships with his mentees cannot stay much better for any extended time.

Mentors who want to be solid leaders and examples to their teams and mentees should make it their business to follow through on the things they commit to themselves, no matter how seemingly trivial, and they should cut out any loopholes they find themselves making. People who sacrifice their integrity for a loophole will generally sacrifice their success and their dreams as well.

Good mentors understand this principle and help their mentees thoroughly grasp it as well.

50

LOVE AND SERVICE

John Burroughs said, "For anything worth having one must pay the price; and the price is always work, patience, love, self-sacrifice—no paper currency, no promises to pay, but the gold of real service." This could easily be the creed of mentoring and leadership. To help his mentee achieve her dream, a mentor must pay a price in hard work, love, and service. Other chapters have focused on the necessity and power of hard work, but this one will discuss the essential nature of love and service.

Mentoring is a process that is intended to build strong relationships along with strong individuals. Mentoring isn't just about the protégé turning out well or the mentor feeding his family. It's about dreams and causes and, therefore, relationships. A mentor who has a huge and glorious dream knows that she can't complete it in full all by herself. She needs friends and allies who can make a difference.

Mentors who have a mentality of service and love for their mentees and act accordingly will increase their love and service. This is one of the greatest secrets of success: as a mentor continually serves his mentee, his love for that mentee and his ability to serve him even better will significantly increase.

An excellent example of this is the father who, rather than lecture or interrogate, focuses on serving his son. As he tries to imagine ways he could make the boy's life better, he builds toward a level of success he never expected.

He finds what he needs to do and does it.

As he stops trying to change his son and instead gives him love and honest service, he finds his anger and frustration slipping away and his love increasing. This doesn't mean to coddle the boy, but rather to care about truly helping him.

And along the way, the father finds something else. As he consistently acts on those little ideas that could make his son's life better, he finds he has more and more of them.

When the mind feels listened to—the feeling that if it suggested something, somebody would care—it starts to speak up louder and stronger. Ideas come all the time, and they become easier to understand.

As the father makes his focus the boy's happiness and not his own fulfillment, he finds he loves him for good reasons. *There are so many reasons!*

Orrin Woodward wrote, "Leadership boils down to the two things that most people cannot resist, love and service." As mentors remember this in their dealings with mentees, they will set an example of true power and leadership.

Service and love not only bring success closer to reality, they also bring a lot of happiness in the moment. A life spent in service and love is usually a life spent with honorable laughter and real happiness.

Mentors who understand the power of service to increase both love and productivity are able to live fuller lives, build stronger relationships with their mentees, and increase their combined influence on the world.

Mentors who also teach their mentees this principle will find a ripple effect of happiness and success.

51

CHALLENGING THE MENTEE

Good mentors know that growth and progress usually come when a person steps outside her comfort zone. As she pushes herself to go beyond the easy stuff and starts working on the hard things, she develops into a stronger, better person. Because of this, mentors are often called upon to challenge their mentees in ways that can be effective, but painful.

Growing is often among the hardest parts of life; it can be challenging and difficult, but it is necessary for success. Mentors should learn to challenge their mentees as often as needed and in many different ways. Frequent challenges in various areas lead to more numerous and increasingly proven strengths for the mentee. Protégés who respond correctly to the mentor's challenges will become more well-rounded themselves as leaders and mentors.

> **Mentors should learn to challenge their mentees as often as needed and in many different ways.**

These challenges can be offered in a number of ways. Perhaps a mentor could assign the mentee to lead a team meeting, to read a tough book, or to reach a high goal in work.

The challenge could even be as simple as a discussion with the mentor himself that challenges the mentee's mind and beliefs in ways that help her become stronger and better. The idea is for the mentor to look for areas that are ready for growth and issue the challenge accordingly.

Pat Riley said, "If you have a positive attitude and constantly strive to give your best effort, eventually you will overcome your immediate problems and find you are ready for greater challenges." As mentors watch this progression, they can be in line to throw the right challenges in at the right times. They should be prayerful and wise in evaluating both the challenges and the responses. Challenges should be well timed and well placed.

This aspect of mentoring is so essential to success that when looking for mentors, people who really hope to be leaders should be sure to plan for it. Author Daniel Coyle said that to find a good mentor, you must "avoid someone who reminds you of a courteous waiter."[35] If the mentor's main goal is to keep his mentees from experiencing any discomfort or difficulty, he will likely not be very helpful to them in their search for success and real happiness.

Courtesy is certainly very important, as was discussed earlier, but mentors who sacrifice excellence for it are not operating at their full potential. Real leaders stand for something big, and they don't allow their desire to be polite or "nice" to stop them from challenging their mentees to do the same.

As mentors challenge their mentees, they will see opportunities to help them grow in meaningful ways, and

they will find that they are issuing challenges to themselves as well, furthering their own growth and progress
as mentors.

52

MENTORING
INITIATIVE

Initiative is one of the most important traits for a real
leader to exhibit, which means that being able to mentor it
is one of the most important tools for a mentor to have.

Bo Bennett said, "Without initiative, leaders are simply
workers in leadership positions." Mentees who haven't
developed initiative usually aren't leaders—they're just
followers. While it's important for leaders to learn to be
good followers in appropriate situations, they shouldn't
be content to be followers at times when they are destined
to be more.

Because initiative is so vital to effective leadership, good
mentors should know how to help their mentees develop
and strengthen this skill.

In order to do this, mentors should start by having a clear
understanding of what initiative really is. Victor Hugo
said, "Initiative is doing the right thing without being
told." In other words, a person of initiative is someone

who sees what needs to be done and does it before he's asked.

The word *initiative* comes from the word *initiate*—to cause or facilitate the beginning of something. Initiative is absolutely a consequence of inspiration. As soon as a mentor requires his mentee to take initiative on this or that, any action the mentee takes is no longer initiative because the mentor already initiated it.

As with other cases of requiring inspired action, the mentor can and should engage the necessity of using initiative in general to promote the success of the mentee. The mentor should help her mentees really understand what initiative is and why it matters. As the mentor does so, and shows her own good example of initiative, the mentee will likely find a growing natural desire to be a person of initiative.

Of course, at the beginning of a mentee's journey to become a person of initiative, the mentor can help the process along in a few ways.

For example, a mentor who is mentoring initiative may want to call her mentee to discuss crises or dilemmas that come up in her business. She can give him the details and ask him to brainstorm solutions. In many situations, there are ways she can even have him help to implement the solutions they come up with. Helping a mentee recognize problems and possible solutions is a great way for a mentor to get him started on the track to real initiative.

Another way mentors can help mentees become people of initiative is to try to explain themselves as often as possible. Naturally, there are times when the mentee will benefit more from waiting for an explanation until after the fact. But in many situations, a mentor can easily explain assignments and instructions so the mentee knows what the mentor is doing and why.

Mentees who understand why a mentor takes a particular action and what things she chooses to do in response to specific issues are already on the path to becoming individuals who see reasons for doing things and are able to choose the right responses.

At some point, the mentor must cut the strings a little. As mentioned, if "initiative" is always initiated by the mentor, the mentor is the only one showing initiative. But if mentors have been inspiring in the right ways and have taught their mentees how to recognize problems and find solutions, they likely won't be disappointed with the mentees' performance when opportunities for initiative arise.

Holbrook Jackson said, "Genius is initiative on fire." As mentors cultivate the initiative of those around them, they will often find the "fire" and energy around them bringing their collective dreams closer to realization. As more leaders with initiative step forward to fight life's battles, great causes will be furthered in stronger ways.

Mentors who help their mentees understand and develop an initiative-based mentality and style will find their own work becoming easier and more effective as others help lift the load. They will also see improvement in the success and leadership abilities of their mentees.

53

MENTORING INGENUITY

Mentoring ingenuity is very similar to mentoring initiative because ingenuity and initiative themselves are very similar. However, as there are subtle differences between the two qualities, there are also subtle differences in the ways mentors pass them on to their mentees.

Ingenuity means accomplishing things in creative and often even bizarre ways. It means doing the job not only well, but with cleverness also. It means overcoming all obstacles by whatever means necessary.

> **Mentors of ingenuity should make it a point to encourage extensive reading.**

Again, this is a skill that can't exactly be required of a person by her mentor—at least not with positive results. But it is also essential to the success of those who wish to be mentors and leaders. Ingenuity (along with tenacity, of course) is one of the most important things that get a dreamer from point A to point B. Without it, real success often isn't found.

A good mentor should set a strong example of ingenuity for his mentees and should help them understand the example they're seeing. Mentees should know what it means to have and use ingenuity because the mentor has

175

both shown them and given them the principles and ideas to correctly interpret the example he sets.

Mentors should give their mentees opportunities to consider solutions to problems and snags. Asking the right questions and allowing mentees to think them through can be a great place to start. However, because of the unique and creative nature of ingenuity, mentors need to add a few other things to their list of mentoring tools. Ingenuity means more than just initiative; it means real genius *in* initiative. To really achieve this, mentors have to take a few extra steps after they've effectively mentored initiative.

For one, mentors of ingenuity should make it a point to encourage extensive reading. Mentees who have read a wide variety and selection of great books by top thinkers are more likely to come up with creative and innovative ideas and answers. If the mentee doesn't have the concepts and ideas in his head, he won't be able to make the necessary connections to come up with the clever ideas that make his initiative *ingenious*. People who read voraciously have much more information to work with as they create solutions and improvements.

Another important element to this part of mentoring is the right kind of confidence. Mentors should help protégés feel confident in bringing solutions to the table. Mentees who are still worried about being laughed out of the room as stupid, naïve, or ridiculous are unlikely to display much ingenuity in their problem-solving journeys. On the other hand, mentees who are confident in their initiative will naturally tend to come up with more creative and outside-the-box solutions.

Mentors should help create an environment where initiative and outside-the-box thinking are encouraged and rewarded. As people become more comfortable with *having* new but amazing ideas, they become much more confident in *sharing* them.

Mentors should help their mentees understand that success includes taking risks and dreaming big. This applies very much to problem solving and all bringing-forth of ideas. Mentors who help their mentees think this way will increase the success and power of their team exponentially. Having a whole team of people thinking independently and ingeniously usually means accomplishing much more than one person ever could on his own as well as more than a team of people following one person's every command and wish could.

> "Never tell people how to do things. Tell them what to do, and they will surprise you with their ingenuity."
> —General George S. Patton

General George S. Patton said, "Never tell people how to do things. Tell them what to do, and they will surprise you with their ingenuity." Mentors and leaders who allow their mentees and associates to think for themselves, rather than expecting them to follow a specific checklist on every detail, are often surprised with the brilliant and unheard-of ways they deal with things. Of course, there is a time and place for a checklist, but mentors should also learn to utilize and encourage the power of ingenuity.

As Bob Richards put it, "Ingenuity, plus courage, plus work, equals miracles." Mentors who teach their mentees these concepts and help them develop these skills will at times see miracles. In history, the impossible has often been achieved by an innovative thinker who was willing to take initiative and use ingenuity to see it through.

Good mentors know that the combination of ingenuity and initiative with hard work and tenacity is truly incredible, and they teach their mentees this lesson through example, experience, and cultivation.

54

GOD AS THE GREATEST MENTOR

Good mentors know that God is ultimately the greatest Mentor, and listening to His guidance and counsel is the best tool for good mentoring. Anytime a mentor has a question about how to help a mentee in a certain way, he can benefit from resorting to prayer. As mentors turn to God for direction and assistance in their mentoring, they are able to more fully recognize and tap in to the special gifts and abilities God has given them.

Just as a mentor who refuses to rely on the help of personal or hero mentors is selling himself short, a mentor who chooses to ignore this vitally important aspect of mentoring is settling for less than both he and his mentees deserve.

In implementing *every* other tool in this book, recognizing God as the greatest Mentor and turning to Him for help will create enormous positive impact. Great mentors understand that God's help is immensely desirable, if not imperative, in the quest for true success and happiness.

As mentors use the power of prayer and turning to God in all things, they should beware of the temptation to expect God to solve all their problems with the snap of His fingers. God is not a genie in a bottle; He isn't just sitting there waiting to grant our various wishes and fulfill our every whim. Mentors shouldn't see God as a way to avoid hard work and real growth; doing so means using God as an excuse to fail, which is, of course, a bad move.

Instead, God frequently supplies His help in the lives of great mentors to help them find the right direction for their hard work. He helps them know the best way to love and serve His children. He can comfort them in failure and help them find new direction. And the list goes on.

Søren Kierkegaard said, "Prayer does not change God, but it changes him who prays."

> **Mentors should never forget that both happiness and success (in the truest sense of the word) depend largely on having the right relationship with God.**

Mentors should think of their interactions with God in this way. They should look to Him as an advisor and a friend— a friend with infinite wisdom and perfect judgment. They should approach prayer not expecting to convince or change God but ready and willing to be convinced and changed themselves.

Mentors should be ready and willing to turn to God in everything. As Corrie ten Boom said, "Any concern too small to be turned into a prayer is too small to be made into a burden." Living a life guided and directed by God will help make a person truly happy. Mentors should never forget that both happiness and success (in the truest sense of the word) depend largely on having the right relationship with God.

This is the most important tool for mentors to internalize and utilize in leadership and mentoring. They should also teach their mentees to do the same.

55

SIMPLICITY ON THE OTHER SIDE OF COMPLEXITY

Simplicity is the ultimate sophistication.
—LEONARDO DA VINCI

Most mentors and mentees who are just starting out tend to focus on the simple things—the basics. They do this because the simple things are brand-new to them.

They're learning and *excited* to be learning. Everything is fresh, and they are totally fired up about the amazing principles and concepts they're discovering. At this stage of their journey, as Confucius

> **"Progress is man's ability to complicate simplicity."**
> **—Thor Heyerdahl**

said, it seems that they "can't open a book [or do much of anything else] without learning something."

Then, after some time and experience, an interesting transition takes place.

Thor Heyerdahl said, "Progress is man's ability to complicate simplicity." At this point, people start to discover deeper and more complex ideas, concepts, and methods, and their focus begins to change. They move past the simple basics and start to learn the harder, more obscure things. They begin pushing the limits of the basics, testing their validity and coming to know the deeper meanings behind them.

Sadly, sometimes mentors and mentees in this stage of development tend to look down on those in the simplicity stage because they consider them "way behind" or think they are "just not getting it." While it isn't a bad thing to be in the complexity stage, it's important that a mentor who *is* in this stage realizes that everyone is at a different level, and the fact that a person isn't learning the same thing he is right now doesn't make that person a loser or a failure. The only losers or failures are those who choose not to learn at all.

After time in this stage, the best mentors should help their mentees and guide them into the next, even higher phase. This next stage is the simplicity on the *other* side of complexity, as Oliver Wendell Holmes put it. Mentors and protégés who make it to this stage have reached a more enlightened and empowered level of learning.

At this phase, they have the new and exciting basics under their belts, as well as the deep thinking and digging into possible meanings and interpretations of the basics. But, at this point, they have come to the realization that it really is all about the basics: doing the basics and doing them *perfectly*.

Chopin said, "Simplicity is the final achievement. After one has played a vast quantity of notes and more notes, it

is simplicity that emerges as the crowning reward of art."
This expresses the point beauti-
fully. Simplicity is the crowning
achievement of art, but only
after a person has been through
the beginning and middle of
the song.

> **"Simplicity is the final achievement. After one has played a vast quantity of notes and more notes, it is simplicity that emerges as the crowning reward of art." —Chopin**

Mentors should under-
stand the excitement of begin-
ners learning the basics. They
should encourage the enthusiasm of each new mentee as
she discovers the basic principles that are about to change
her life. They should suggest resources and add insights to
help mentees get the most out of their study of the basics.

Mentors should also know and feel the importance of
digging into the complex pieces of the great ideas. The
mentor should be there with her mentee to push him to
dig even deeper. She should suggest readings and discussions that will challenge him even further to grasp the
complexity. Of course, as she does this, she should remind
him always to be humble and loving toward those with
whom he interacts. Becoming arrogant about being in
the complexity stage is not particularly supportive to
successful leadership or mentoring.

Ultimately, however, mentors should remember that
the simplicity on the other side of complexity—getting
back to the basics with full understanding and mastery—
is the real goal. The mentor should help her mentees work

toward this end and help them avoid getting trapped in complexity mode or giving up along the way.

Understanding what the real end goal is—that simplicity and mastery of the basics is really a position of power and inspiration—is vitally important to good mentoring. Mentees should seek out mentors who really understand the power of fundamentals and love teaching them.[36]

Mentors should use this knowledge and understanding to improve their ability to give meaningful mentoring.

As a mentor recognizes what stage his mentee is in, he is able to target the focus and method of his mentoring to the needs of the mentee. He also increases his ability to inspire mentees and set a good example.

56

MENTORING TENACITY, RESILIENCE, AND ENDURANCE

Tenacity, resilience, and endurance are three of the most important traits of real leadership, so mentors should be very familiar with them and help their mentees develop them. People who have these qualities are more likely to achieve real success and happiness than those who don't.

TENACITY

Tenacity has been discussed in previous chapters, but it is absolutely key that mentors and mentees develop it if they want to turn their dreams into realities.

Albert Einstein, who is known for being a genius, said, "Genius is 1 percent talent and 99 percent hard work." And Thomas Edison, who is known for never giving up, said, "Many of life's failures are people who did not realize how close they were to success when they gave up."

These men knew what they were talking about because they lived it. They knew what they were talking about, and they were right.

So how does a mentor actually mentor this attribute once he understands it? There are three main ways, and they should all be used in conjunction with each other.

> **Mentors should help their mentees consciously choose tenacity at every opportunity.**

1. *Example.* Mentees who have a tenacious mentor to look up to often find it easier to create and sustain a drive within themselves. Mentors should help create an environment that naturally attracts and cultivates real tenacity.

2. *Principles.* Mentees who have been taught the value and importance of tenacity are more likely to do the work when it gets hard than those who have not. Mentors should make sure

their mentees truly understand how essential and powerful tenacity really is.

3. *Experience.* Mentees who have been showered with little experiences that helped and expected them to make the tenacious choice will be more able to choose it when the really hard times come.

Mentors should find times and ways to help their mentees test and exercise their tenacity. It should be a constant conversation between them, so everyone knows what's going on. But mentors should challenge and test mentees in ways that *push* them—and at times, push them hard. Mentees should always be in practice.

This doesn't mean the mentor needs to throw setbacks at the mentee so she can practice working harder. What it does mean is that when those setbacks and hard times come—and they will—the mentor talks the mentee through them and helps her to recognize her choice. Mentors should help their mentees consciously choose tenacity at every opportunity.

RESILIENCE

Resilience is the strength to avoid being broken and to bounce back after being bent. It is the quality that helps mentors and mentees see failures as opportunities and defeats as lessons instead of being stopped or destroyed by either one.

Jodi Picoult said, "The human capacity for burden is like bamboo—far more flexible than you'd ever believe at first glance."[37] Mentors can help their mentees realize this and tap into that "human capacity" when it really matters. Interestingly, the ways a mentor can teach resilience are pretty much the same as those for teaching tenacity:

4. *Example.* Mentees who see their mentor bouncing back from the most difficult challenges in life are generally empowered. The strong example lets them know they can do it too. If the mentor can survive such a setback, so can the mentee. Mentors should be a constant example of resilience to their mentees, an example they can identify and understand.

5. *Principles.* Mentees who have been taught that resilience is power—the power to make it to their dreams—often find the strength to follow the example set by their mentors because they understand the *why* of it. Mentors should make sure their mentees know what it means to be resilient and why they should even care about it. Knowing what makes something important helps people make the choice to do it.

6. *Experience.* Mentees who can point to specific past experiences of their own resilience are more likely to believe in their power to be resilient *today.* Every time a mentee experiences what it feels like to be resilient, his mentor should

make sure he really understands what he did. Mentors who do this will have their mentees saying, "I've done it before, and because it matters to me, I will do it again."

ENDURANCE

These three traits build on one another. Tenacity is the hard work that gets you on the path to greatness. Once you're on that path, you make enemies and face obstacles, and these can bring you down. That's why you need resilience: to get back up, brush off the dust, and keep walking. Endurance is the thing inside that says, after every bout of resilience almost drains a person, "It's all worth it, and no matter what, I will *not* give up—not ever." It's the thing that *says* that, and it's also the thing that *does* it.

Virgil wrote, "Come what may, all bad things are to be overcome by endurance." In the final analysis, endurance is a combination of tenacity and resilience, and it is absolutely essential to success.

Mentors should teach endurance using the powerful tools of *example*, *principle*, and *experience*. And they should do so prayerfully because this is a message that, though hard to receive, is absolutely necessary.

Mentors should remember that endurance—the duo of tenacity and resilience, extended over a lifetime—is essential on the path to success, happiness, and impact.

57

THE POWER OF IDEAS IN MENTORING

Good mentors recognize that ideas have power. Orrin Woodward said, "Ideas have enormous consequence in a person's life because you ultimately become what you believe." Often what a person really believes he is, he actually becomes. Mentors need to be aware of their deepest beliefs because they will impact the way their lives turn out.

One interesting literary example of this comes from the popular Broadway musical *Wicked*. The whole story is about a girl with high hopes and dreams and good solid morals. The only problem—she's green. Yes, for some reason, Elphaba was born with green skin.

She has a very good and generous heart, but she's been raised around people who believe her green skin is a sign of evil. So, she goes through life hoping big but genuinely believing that, unless the Wizard of Oz magically changes her into something normal, she can never be beautiful, happy, or even good.

Many people wonder how the kind, sweet girl from *Wicked* turns into the wicked witch we know from the 1939 film *The Wizard of Oz*. She's not only the most *good* person in the play; she's also the smartest and the most tenacious as well. Even at the end of the musical, the audience isn't left thinking she's evil, only that she refuses to accept limits just because people say they're there. She finishes the play by saying she will try to change the world—to make it better.

So how does this real gem turn into the witch we all know?

Unfortunately, somewhere along the way, she starts to believe the opinions others have of her; she starts to believe she must really be evil. That is the beginning of the end for her.

As this young woman tries to do right, she constantly undercuts herself by believing she must harbor an evil motive. She allows herself to compromise things that she shouldn't because she *believes* it is beyond her control to choose bad *or* good.

She fosters this idea of who she is, and in so doing, she allows herself to become the Wicked Witch of the West—a person who is *actually* wicked.

This is a tragic tale, especially for those who experience the musical and come to understand the powerful force for good that this unfortunate young woman *could* have been.

Now, imagine if she had a good mentor. Of course, he could not change her beliefs for her, but the right wisdom from a trusted and excellent mentor can make a world of difference in a person's life. What would *The Wizard of Oz* have been with an Elphaba the Good?

Sadly, too many people allow themselves to get caught up in "the way things are" instead of making them the way they should be. This is one area in which mentors can greatly assist a mentee. A good mentor should always try to be aware of her mentee's beliefs because her wisdom can really change things for him in this respect.

Woodward reminds leaders how important it is not to waste tomorrow on yesterday. Most likely every mentee who comes to a mentor will have limiting beliefs because of past experience and hardship. This is a simple reality. But one of the most powerful tools in a mentor's bag is the ability to reframe the mentee's false beliefs.

There are a number of ways to do this, and mentors should target their methods to the readiness and openness of the individual mentee. The chapters entitled "How (and When) to Reprimand," "Ask Yourself Questions," and "How to Use Archetypes" can be helpful in developing this process outlined below:

1. Know your mentee's views of himself by having him do the archetype exercise and share his results with you, where appropriate.

2. Use the questions from the other two chapters mentioned above to get an idea of his reality and his potential, as well as the best course of action for you to help him with reframing.

Good mentors should remember tact and love. Don't overwhelm the mentee; that will likely make the situation worse. Be honest, sincere, loving, and trust-worthy throughout the process.

A mentor who came to young Elphaba's rescue, one who knew her well enough to help her see the choice she had to make, show her the happy future and wonderful influence she was capable of, and assist her in making the choice and acting on it could have changed the entire history of Oz, not to mention the happiness of a once sweet and caring girl.

Interestingly, this is also how *The Wizard of Oz* ends. Dorothy begins with false beliefs about herself and what she can accomplish; she feels like the victim of a boring life in Kansas and then powerless to return home from Oz. She also has high hopes that the wizard will magically solve all her problems and make her the person she wants to be. And, of course, she is also ultimately disappointed in his ability to make her successful.

This is where the main difference occurs. At this point, Dorothy has a wise and loving mentor, Glenda the Good, who comes in and helps her see reality. Dorothy has all the power to make her dreams come true, and she has *always* had it.

> **Mentors who help their mentees reframe their false beliefs are *literally* helping them reframe their futures.**

Dorothy's reframing is a bit simplified, but it does happen. Dorothy changes her limiting beliefs with the help and guidance of a great mentor, and she finds happiness and success.

Even back in Kansas, she finds ways to control her beliefs and her outlook on life and is able to be happy in a world that at first seemed black and white and dull.

This is a poignant example of the difference a good mentor can make in the future of his mentee by helping her foster the right kind of ideas and beliefs—especially self-beliefs. Mentors who help their mentees reframe their false beliefs are *literally* helping them reframe their futures.

58

THE POWER OF EMULATION

Every person who wants to be successful should understand the power of emulation. Sowing wild oats or trying to see how many crazy, rebellious, or completely bizarre things you can accomplish in life is not a good approach to business or mentoring. Mentors should look at the successful systems that are in place in their company or organization and put them to good use in their mentoring. Mentors who mean to achieve their dreams understand that they can't do everything by themselves. If a mentor goes through life trying to make up his own ways to do everything and ignores the trails blazed by the mentors and leaders who went before him, he is not optimizing his time and effort. He makes more work for himself, wastes more time on trial and error, and ultimately accomplishes less. If he knows that something works, it's folly for him to try everything else, just in case he knows better than everyone else.

The power of emulation is learning from people who know how to do something and then following their systems and methods. Mentors should teach their mentees this skill and help them understand its value.

> **Effective initiative and innovation build on the foundation of well-conceived methods and systems.**

Mentees who learn this principle and implement it will usually find that their work more quickly progresses toward something meaningful. Mentees who run around trying everything but the proven system often waste time and energy trying to climb empty trees. Their focus goes in so many wrong directions that it gets them nothing because they never crack down and get started on their real path.

In this case, conformity is the solution. Mentors and mentees should conform to the preset, tried-and-true systems in their organizations, not because they're systems but because they *work*. This is the difference between conformity for conformity's sake and conformity for the sake of rightness and success.

Chris Brady said, "Anything worth doing well is worth doing poorly until you can master it." While this is true, it is important for mentors and mentees to remember that the ultimate goal is not to be "the king of discovery," but to do the thing *well*. Brady also said, "The best experience is someone else's, properly examined and applied." Properly emulating the methods set by people who have achieved success is the smart way to go about life. Effective initiative and innovation build on the foundation of well-conceived methods and systems. There's no need to waste time and energy on reinventing simply to reinvent.

Buddha put it well when he said, "Follow then the shining ones, the wise, the awakened, the loving, for they know how to work and forbear." Following the examples and advice of people who have tried various ways of doing things and found the best one is harnessing the power of emulation. These people not only know how to work hard and forbear, they also know where and how to work hard and forbear in order to achieve the greatest results.

Focusing on the right action is much better than doing double or triple the work on a million things that don't get the desired results. In fact, many people never find success because they try to spread their hard work over too many undertakings. The power of emulation has a lot to do with the power of focus—it's about focusing hard work on the right things, instead of just working for the sake of doing work.

Just as conformity is not a virtue for its own sake but for the virtue of the thing conformed to, hard work is not a virtue for *its* own sake but for the thing it is directed at and

> **Emulation is about conforming to the right methods, so the hard work goes toward the right things.**

the goals it accomplishes. Emulation is about conforming to the right methods, so the hard work goes toward the right things.

Of course, mentors should advise their mentees to be careful who they emulate. They should follow dedicated and successful leaders, not evil or ignorant men. As mentors share the importance of emulation, they should guide their mentees to the right principles, systems, and experts, so they're sure to emulate the right things.

Mentors who help their teams understand the power of emulation will find their success exponentially increased as more and more protégés start emulating the right procedures and making their hard work count.

59

REFRAMING CHALLENGES

Just as good mentors reframe their mentees' dreams and beliefs, they should also reframe their mentees' challenges. Often, mentees are caught up and blinded by challenges that seem too big to approach, let alone overcome. At these times, mentors can be a great help by stepping in and reframing the challenges to fit into the mentees' realm of what's even possible.

Mentors should help mentees see ways they can bite off smaller, more manageable chunks of the challenge to work on right now, instead of letting them stay trapped in the mentality of overwhelming helplessness.

One mentor shared the following story about this concept:

I have this one mentee, a really sharp and dedicated woman, but one who tends to get overwhelmed by challenges, to the point that she has a very difficult time moving forward when faced with a big one.

What I've learned as I've tried to help her through these struggles is that she just needs to be told she can do it, and then she has to *start working*. When I first began working with her, she would call me quite often, totally scared stiff by some obstacle that seemed too big to be surmounted.

When she would call, I would calm her down and ask, "What is the problem?" After she explained it all to me, I had a follow-up question already prepared: "So, what's the first thing you can do to make a dent in it?"

As we got used to this routine, she started to laugh at herself right about here, and eventually she got to the point where she just reframed her challenges herself.

The key to solving unsolvable problems is to make them into ten, or a hundred, or a million—however many it takes—smaller but *totally* solvable problems, and then to tackle number one, number two, number three. However many little battles and triumphs it takes to achieve the final big triumph of having tackled the challenge and won, it is totally worth it.

It is important for mentors to recognize and validate big challenges, but then they need to get the mentee moving. Sitting around staring at the impossibility of the thing will only make a mentee feel less able. Incidentally, this is the same way to teach a four-year-old (or a sixteen-year-old) to clean a bedroom.

Mentors should help mentees stop looking at the whole forest and start noticing the first tree. Mentors should be encouraging and reassuring. They should let the mentee know how much they believe in her ability to get through the test with flying colors.

As mentors apply this principle of looking at both the big picture and the next step in every aspect of mentoring, their mentees will learn to do the same, and the mentors will promote valuable action in their mentees, rather than endless evaluation or frustration.

60

YES, NO, MAYBE, LATER, AND RIGHT NOW

Good mentors should learn when to say yes, and when to say no. Additionally this includes knowing how and when to say "later" and "right now."

Mentors can build the confidence and initiative of mentees by accepting their proposals, suggestions, and requests. This is an important part of mentoring that helps mentees learn to think for themselves and direct their own projects.

Ultimately, mentors want their mentees to become strong and powerful leaders themselves, rather than staying in the nest forever. Saying yes at appropriate times is a great way to help mentees develop this independence and personal direction. A mentor should try to say yes as often as possible in regard to a mentee's life or stewardship because it gives the mentee the opportunity to be responsible for herself and her work—to feel that she makes her own choices with the support of her mentor.

On the other hand, mentors should not say yes just for the sake of it, or out of habit. As Gandhi said, "A 'No' uttered from the deepest conviction is better than a 'Yes' merely uttered to please, or worse, to avoid trouble."

In fact, mentees often learn a lot from being told no by their mentor. Being told that this time they need to follow instead of doing their own thing is one of the most powerful lessons in the experience of mentees.

Sometimes a mentor must reject proposals or requests made by his mentee because his wisdom and experience allow him to see the situation differently. Either the situation needs something else, or the mentee does. In either case, saying no at these times is vitally important to the success and growth of the mentee.

Mentors should be careful about using the word *maybe*. Often in modern English, people use this word to softly say no without seeming too harsh or negative. The problem is that's not actually what the word means. The word is meant to express indecision or ignorance about future possibilities. "Maybe" means "I haven't decided yet" or "I don't know yet"; it could be either yes or no.

Mentors should avoid using *maybe* in the popular way (the *no* with removed responsibility). Real leaders say what they mean and take responsibility for their words. A mentor who says no when he means to and owns it is much more effective and respectable than one who tries to let the mentee down easy, attempting all the while to look innocent and agreeable.

> **Real leaders say what they mean and take responsibility for their words.**

The more technical usage is slightly better, but still to be avoided by real leaders and good mentors. It is okay and even powerful for a mentor to admit he doesn't know everything, but he shouldn't hide behind the word to excuse himself from finding out or deciding, any more than he should hide behind it to seem pleasant.

George Canning said, "Indecision and delays are the parents of failure." The word *maybe* as indecision or delay is dangerous because it puts the mentor into a victim mentality, which always leads to failure if it isn't corrected. Mentors should make a point of either knowing whether the answer is yes or no or else deciding, when that's what the circumstances require.

The right way to get the only good sentiments of the word *maybe* into mentoring is using the word *later*. While it's seldom a good thing for a mentor to be indecisive or ignorant, often a mentor who knows his own mind and understands the situation will know that now isn't the right time.

Telling the mentee to wait before implementing, studying, or attempting something she isn't ready for is an important role for good mentors to play. Mentors have more experience and have often been in the mentee's shoes before, so being able to tell the mentee to hold off on something beyond her is hugely beneficial.

Tackling the hardest, biggest challenges of life is almost always more effective if it comes with a significant amount of previous training. Mentors should teach their mentees the importance of patience. Achieving their dreams is not something they will be able to do overnight. Patience means working at things and accepting that results don't always come according to your schedule. But it also means waiting to tackle certain challenges or seek out certain experiences until you're ready to overcome and optimize them.

Mentors who tell their mentees "later" and teach them these principles can save them a lot of grief and extra work. Doing things in their proper place and at their proper time is very important to progress and success.

In all this, mentors should help mentees recognize the difference between patience and procrastination, which brings us to our next point.

Sometimes a mentor must step in and say "right now." Occasionally, mentees will get stuck in past routines and fail to recognize the need for change or additional action. They may believe it would be best for them to continue what they're doing currently rather than implement some new ideas or systems. In these cases, a mentor saying "right now" can be what they need to avoid stagnation and choose growth.

Mentors should be loving and kind about the way they use "right now," but they should not be afraid to do so. Sometimes tough love is exactly what mentees need, and often their success depends on the right push from their mentor.

Mentors should understand the necessity of each of these answers and balance them appropriately. A mentor who teaches his mentees about these different responses will help them in their own mentoring and also improve their reception of his counsel and advice, especially when it isn't the easiest to swallow.

61

How to Customize Your Mentoring

Good mentors don't assume that each of their mentees should be treated in the same manner—they personalize their mentoring. Getting to know each mentee individually can really help in this process. Knowing a mentee's love language, dreams, fears, strengths, and weaknesses will help the mentor to give the right kind of mentoring and fit the relationship to the mentee's specific needs.

Mentoring is ineffective if the mentee isn't learning or growing from it, so mentors should learn how to teach in a way that gets through to the individual mentee. And because everyone is different, this will mean several different styles and methods of mentoring. Mentors who are able to adapt to the needs of each mentee will be able to help many people from different backgrounds and with different life missions. Mentors who don't may be able to help one or two who happen to fit their particular style, but they will have significantly smaller impact than those who are more adaptable.

David Bailey, who is often considered to be one of Britain's best photographers, said, "You adapt to who you're photographing." The reason for this is that different people will look better and more themselves in different lighting or locations. Additionally, different people will appear at best advantage from different angles and in different poses. Photographers who understand this are able to come out with better pictures and happier subjects.

> **Mentoring is ineffective if the mentee isn't learning or growing from it, so mentors should learn how to teach in a way that gets through to the individual mentee.**

Not every person can pull off a straight-on, full-toothed smile. Many will be better and happier with a side angle and a shy half smile. This is a reality. Because people have different faces, expressions, and personalities, they need a photographer who can give them a different approach based on what's best for each individual.

This same principle applies to mentoring.

One of the most basic ways for a mentor to customize his mentoring to an individual is to work out a program *with* the mentee herself. At the beginning of the mentoring relationship, after the mentor has asked the right questions and feels he knows the mentee well enough to continue, it is a good idea for the mentor to ask his mentee to make a list of what she wants from the relationship and specifically from the mentor. She should include her own goals and dreams and how she hopes the mentor can help her get closer to achieving them.

While the mentee is doing this, the mentor should make his own list. Based on the mentoring questions he's asked about the mentee, he should make an outline of things he thinks he has to offer her. He should include his own goals and suggestions for what he thinks the mentee should expect and hope to get from the relationship.

When both have their lists, the two can meet together and discuss what they came up with. The mentor should remember that this is all ultimately the mentee's life, not his own, and act accordingly. He should not try to push the mentee too hard to be what *he* wants her to be, but he can and should let the mentee know if he feels strongly about some difference in their visions. After all, the mentee came to a mentor because she recognized her need for help and guidance.

> **Once a mentor knows what the mentee is actually looking for from him, customizing his mentoring is a matter of getting to know the mentee's personality, communication style, and learning style, along with her strengths and weaknesses.**

Having a mutual understanding and agreement of what each party wants and expects from the relationship can remove certain doubts, questions, and conflicts from the relationship. Mentors and mentees should both keep a written copy of the understanding they came to, so they'll have it to turn to whenever they want.

Once a mentor knows what the mentee is actually looking for from him, customizing his mentoring is a matter of getting to know the mentee's personality, communication style, and learning style, along with her strengths and weaknesses. Once he knows these, he can tailor his service to the mentee.

As the relationship grows and parties learn more and more about each other, mentors will be able to adapt their style even more to the mentee's, and vice versa, and the effectiveness of their interactions will increase.

As mentors grow and experience more personalities and styles, they will become better at recognizing the specific needs of each new mentee, and effective mentoring relationships will develop more rapidly. In this sense, mentoring is a matter of practice. Once the mentor understands the principles behind customized mentoring, he just needs to start working on it. Then with experience comes mastery.

So, to customize mentoring to each individual mentee:

1. Know the mentee.
2. Know what the mentee wants from the relationship.
3. Get to work.
4. Learn more about the mentee as you go along, and adapt accordingly.
5. Keep practicing.

206

Mentors who do this will increase the scope and strength of their influence. And of course, teaching their mentees to do the same in *their* mentoring will increase the influence even more.

62

MENTORING WITH SPECIFIC INTENT

Along with customized mentoring, mentoring with specific intent can be a great way for mentors and mentees to focus their efforts on work that goes toward what they are trying to accomplish. Peter Marshall said, "God will not permit any troubles to come upon us, unless He has a specific plan by which great blessing can come out of the difficulty."

Mentors should try to emulate this aspect of God. They should not create extra or meaningless work or trouble for their mentees. Work and difficulty should be aimed at a specific target, for a specific purpose, and to achieve specific results.

To develop the point further, not only should mentors *not* create extra work without specific intent, they should make sure that everything they assign or request is meaningful and to the point. There should be an intended and monitored lesson or goal in every assignment and job mentees are given.

This is not to say that the mentees can't or won't learn many other lessons and principles as they do these specific assignments—in fact, they probably will—but mentors shouldn't trust in the *probably* to make it meaningful. They should know that it matters, and why, before they ask for it.

The reason this matters so much is that working to achieve a specific intention allows mentors and mentees to narrow in their focus and give 100 percent to seeing it finished. People who work with specific intent are able to bring their passion, conviction, tenacity, and talent together to make things happen, while those who feel their tasks are meaningless are likely to give them only a fraction of their focus, and ultimately a half-hearted effort results in a half-done job.

Wayne Dyer said, "Our intention creates our reality." While people often take action based on intentions, which they then fail to realize, this statement still holds true over time. One action may have results that belie its intention, but if different actions are taken again and again stemming from the same intention, the person taking them will see a definite bend toward the achievement, whether or not she occasionally takes an accidental step in the wrong direction.

Mentors should know that the meaning behind every action defines the action itself. For this reason, every action should be pointed toward the right result—the achievement of one's dream.

Specific intent is akin to focus. It means consciously choosing *only* those actions and behaviors that get a person closer to his goal. The biggest part of achieving this in mentoring is simply remembering the principle and choosing to implement it. As usual, it's all about just doing it! However, there are a few techniques that can help mentors with this.

First, mentors should make a point of clearly defining intentions. Knowing what he's working toward will help the mentor immensely in targeting his assignments and mentoring toward it. To figure out intentions, mentors should repeat the exercise in the previous chapter on customized mentoring. They should make a list of what they hope to achieve through each mentoring relationship and have their mentees do the same. Then they should meet together and clarify their joint vision and intention. This will help mentors and mentees stay on the same page so they can avoid unnecessary confusion.

Second, mentors can make a habit of asking themselves a few questions before they give an assignment or move in a new direction. Some examples of the right questions to ask are as follows:

1. What is our shared vision of what we ultimately hope to accomplish?
2. What is my intention with this specific action?
3. Does my intention move us closer to accomplishing our vision?

4. With this information, is there any way I need to reframe my intention or change my planned action?

5. Now that I have these answers, should I take this action or make this assignment?

Asking these five questions (and others like them) before acting can be a very powerful way to mentor with specific intent.

Mentors should tell their mentees to expect specific-intent mentoring, rather than beat-around-the-bush or wild-goose-chase mentoring.

63

RECOGNITION

Good mentors know that distinction and recognition are very powerful motivations for most mentees. Recognition is similar to praise, but it goes a step beyond. Praise is more about the words a mentor gives in private or in public that let the mentee know her good work or behavior has been noticed and appreciated. Of course, praise is a form of recognition, but there are also many other forms and levels of recognition that are equally as important as praise, if not more so.

Recognition also includes more substantial rewards such as promotion, pay raise, increased attention from superiors, extra mentoring, and increased leadership opportunities and responsibilities. In organizations that value leadership and excellence, it is important to recognize and reward those qualities. As mentees see real achievement

> **In organizations that value leadership and excellence, it is important to recognize and reward those qualities.**

bringing real rewards, they will be motivated to work hard toward those achievements and rewards.

As Orrin Woodward stated in his discussion of The Five Laws of Decline in his book *RESOLVED*, men tend to want to get the most benefit for the least amount of work, which often leads to plunder.

When mentors and organizations aren't careful to give deserved recognition to the right people, they can actually make the effects of this human tendency worse. If people who work hard and accomplish things aren't given recognition for their contributions, then people who are lazy, unskilled, and unhelpful will be receiving the same treatment as the ones who do all the work.

This is very destructive to productivity and progress because if people can receive the same benefit from living the easy life as they can from tenaciously working through the night to accomplish their dreams, very few will be motivated enough to pick the second option. Many of those who *do* try will likely have their spirit broken in the process.

As Bob Nelson said, "People may take a job for more money, but they often leave it for more recognition." Mentors should understand that for people who are on the path to success, the right kind of recognition is sometimes more important than money or security. People want to work for a purpose and to achieve a dream, so if they don't see those growing closer, it may not matter what you're offering in their place.

Mentors should learn to recognize achievement and excellence in their mentees. Recognize by (1) seeing and (2) doing something about it.

Sometimes this is as simple as a praising, but when the achievement requires more, mentors should be ready and happy to give it. Mentors need to match the size of the recognition to the size of the accomplishment—and then give it without holding back. In these situations, mentees should always know that they're being recognized and why.

Mentors who do this will create positive attitudes in their mentees and an environment where mentees strive harder to perform at their very best levels in everything they do.

64

MENTORING ACCOUNTABILITY AND RESPONSIBILITY

Good mentors hold their protégés accountable and get them to take responsibility. Real leaders know they are accountable for their own actions and behaviors; they take responsibility when they fail and do their best to right past wrongs.

When mentees work in an environment where they are given tangible and deserved recognition, they are already beginning the process of learning to take responsibility for both their successes and their failures. Mentors who are known to give recognition when recognition is due are more able to effectively crack down on mentees when their actions or behaviors produce less-encouraged results.

Taking responsibility and taking steps to make things right are some of the most vital actions of any great leader. Chris Brady said, "Leaders are givers and takers: givers of credit and takers of responsibility and blame." Mentors should teach their mentees to know when they are at fault, admit it, and make it right.

After mentors have explained these concepts to their mentees, the example they set is extremely important. Mentees should see their mentors giving credit to those who deserve it and admitting their own failings when they mess up. Seeing a good example of such maturity and leadership usually makes the choice to act maturely a lot easier for mentees.

That said, it is important that mentees look to more than just the past. Knowing he will be the one to receive the consequence for his choices—reward or punishment—will help the mentee not only hold himself accountable for what he has done but also take responsibility for what he must do in order to achieve his own future success. As George Bernard Shaw said, "We are made wise not by the recollection of our past, but by the responsibility for our future."

> **Taking responsibility and taking steps to make things right are some of the most vital actions of any great leader.**

By rewarding mentees for right and good behaviors and setting the example of how to take responsibility for failures as well, mentors will help mentees become accountable. This will make them more powerful because when they know there's no one to blame or congratulate but themselves, mentees are more likely to make the right choice.

65

MENTORING BALANCE

Good mentors help mentees develop balance. Drive and business are not the only vital factors in their success. There is more to the dreams of most mentees than mere financial success. They generally also have important visions of what their family life should look like, what kind of friendships they want to have, which personal attributes they want to develop, and what spiritual or religious goals they want to accomplish.

As mentors push mentees to be stronger and more successful in certain areas of life, they should not encourage them to neglect others. Zig Ziglar said, "I believe that being successful means having a balance of success stories across the many areas of your life. You can't truly be considered successful in your business life if your home life is in shambles."

Success in business and leadership absolutely does not require failure in marriage or parenthood. In fact, the only failure that success requires is the failure to choose failure. It is totally possible for a person to put the necessary effort and tenacity into his work without compromising the other things that really matter.

In reality, in achieving their dreams, leaders will find that getting the family on board and tuned in to their vision will strengthen rather than weaken their ability to do what it takes.

> **It is totally possible for a person to put the necessary effort and tenacity into his work without compromising the other things that really matter.**

Those who feel they are sacrificing too much for their business are usually not sacrificing enough—they're just sacrificing the wrong things. Mentors should know that to achieve real success and happiness, people *must* be willing to find the right balance in their lives.

Philip Green said, "It's all about quality of life and finding a happy balance between work and friends and family." Often people mistakenly believe that this means breaking up their focus and giving halfhearted efforts in each area of life. Mentors should help their mentees see that this is not true.

In the first place, leaders should share their enthusiasm and vision with their family and friends. Often, when a person takes the time to tell his family what he's doing and why it matters so much to him and then *asks* them to join him in sacrificing for it, he finds that they respect him and love him for his dedication to his dream, instead of feeling resentful for every minute of time he isn't spending with them.

When a person shares his dream, its meaning, and his dedication and invites his wife and children to support and help him in it, they are often inspired and excited. By explaining and inviting, rather than ignoring and

216

informing, he gives them the opportunity to act because they *want* to, which makes their actions much more meaningful and powerful.

Leaders—wherever they are on their journey, whether new mentee or seasoned mentor—should make a point of setting aside special time to spend with their family. And when they're with their family, it should be *all* about family. This is a time to show them the love and attention they need and deserve.

Families who feel like they are given all of you when it's their turn will be happier to let you go all in when it's somebody else's. By the same token, when it's time to be working on the business or in the community or for church, real leaders should be 100 percent present and focused there as well.

On top of all this, mentors should instruct their mentees to be prayerful about how they structure their time and where they direct their attention. They should always be aware of the needs of the different aspects of their dreams and should learn to balance the different parts of their life. Mentors should constantly remind their mentees about the importance of balance to success and should help them foster a healthy balance in their businesses, homes, and marriages.

66

WHEN TO ASK, WHEN TO TELL, AND WHEN TO ASSIGN

Good mentors should maintain a proper balance of asking, telling, and assigning. Depending on which they use, the tone and nature of the communication will be very different. Knowing which one to use in each situation will have a huge impact on the mentor's ability to optimize her influence with mentees.

Asking a mentee if he will do something, rather than telling him to or assigning it, can be a great way to build the mentee's accountability, responsibility, and independence. Mentors who respect their mentee's right to choose action for himself will usually win points with him for doing so—and not just in the "you're a cool person" way, but also in the "I know I can trust you because you treat me like a person" way. These are the kinds of "points" that strengthen the relationship and increase the mentor's influence.

This also gives the mentee good practice in making decisions that build his confidence and strengthen his drive to act on his own. Mentors should make a habit of asking, instead of telling, whenever the circumstances allow.

In this, however, it is important for mentors to remember that if they *ask* for something, rather than assigning or telling, they have left the mentee with the option to say no. There will eventually be something where the mentor can't afford a "no" answer from the mentee, and in those cases, she should not ask but use another method.

Often, even though the mentor would prefer a yes, she should leave it open for the mentee's decision. When a mentee says no, mentors should take time to express their reason for the request and then ask again. If the mentee still says no, the mentor should respect his choice and move on.

> **Mentees who are allowed to make their own decisions learn what it means to be strong leaders.**

Part of the power of asking is that it does leave the outcome up to the mentee. Mentors should do their best to inspire the mentee to give the answer they feel is best for him by explaining how they came to their conclusions. But ultimately it's up to him, and they shouldn't require acquiescence.

As mentioned, mentors should use asking—as opposed to telling or assigning—as often as possible, since it is the most conducive to authentic leadership and success.

Telling, on the other hand, should be used very sparingly, if ever—especially with more advanced protégés. As protégés develop and grow, the need for them to make their own decisions in nearly every case increases. As long as a mentee is answering to commands from the emperor-mentor, he is not standing entirely on his own two feet.

Mentees who are allowed to make their own decisions learn what it means to be strong leaders, while those who are tied to their mentor's apron strings are held back because they are not yet fully responsible for their actions. Telling shifts accountability from the shoulders of the mentee to those of the mentor: if the mentor makes the decision and causes the action, she is responsible for a good portion of the outcome.

Telling is *requiring*, and while it has its place, that place is very small and infrequently needed. The reason telling is so dangerous is that in most mentoring cases, it relies on false authority. The mentor is the boss, so what she says goes; the mentee's life and future are in the mentor's control.

> **Assignments come, not from what a mentor can hold over the mentee's head to force him into action, but from the natural state of a mentor-to-mentee relationship.**

However, there are times when a mentor shouldn't leave so much to chance by asking weak questions. There will be times when she will feel the mentee really ought to do a thing no matter what. In these situations, the mentor should usually resort to an assignment. Assignments are the positive version of telling—stronger than a question, but still respectful of individual responsibility and choice.

Assignments come, not from what a mentor can hold over the mentee's head to force him into action, but from the natural state of a mentor-to-mentee relationship. An understood and vital part of mentoring is the giving and accepting of assignments by mentors and mentees respectively.

Of course, a mentee still has the option to decline an assignment, but in the right kind of relationship, this is rare. Mentors who rely mostly on asking to inspire action from their mentees generally build their trust to the point that when assignments do come, the mentee recognizes their importance and jumps to fulfill them because he knows it's probably exactly what he needs.

Mentors who have a clear and right understanding of authority and only use it in healthy and appropriate ways will gain the respect from their mentees that makes all the difference when they do extend an assignment.

Mentors who correctly use these ways of getting a mentee to do something will find themselves building stronger leaders and getting closer to overall success.

67

THE EMPLOYEE VERSUS THE ENTREPRENEURIAL MIND-SET

Mentors should help their mentees get out of an employee mind-set and into an entrepreneurial one. This often means the difference between failure and success in people's lives, so understanding it is very important for mentors.

The difference between employee mind-sets and entre-preneurial mind-sets is that one leads to sitting around waiting to be told what to do and never initiates much in life, while the other leads to initiative, ingenuity, and innovation and ultimately to progress, recognition, and increased success.

It is important to note that "employee mind-set" doesn't have to be the default setting of anyone who happens to be an employee. Quite the contrary. Employees can and should be successful leaders in their sphere, just like everyone else. The thing that makes the difference between an employee–leader and a plain old employee is an entre-preneurial mind-set.

Real leaders have an entrepreneurial view of themselves and the world. They are constantly looking for creative new ways to improve their situation and the world around them. Peter Drucker said, "The entrepreneur always searches for change, responds to it, and exploits it as an opportunity."[38] Mentors should teach their mentees that whatever their circumstances, adopting an entrepreneurial mind-set will help them optimize their results and bring them closer to success.

We've already discussed the power of beliefs, as well as the power of focus. Entrepreneurial mind-set is all about fostering the right beliefs and focusing on the right things. Mentors should help their mentees believe in their ability to accomplish great and powerful things and encourage them to focus on positive and innovative solutions to every problem or question.

An excellent example of this is in the 2005 film *Robots*. The main character, a young inventor, is always coming up with new gadgets to help improve his family's circumstances or his father's work. He goes around repeating the words, "See a need; fill a need." He got this motto from his hero, big-time inventor Bigweld, who is his inspiration.

One evening, he sees his dad (who is a dishwasher at a local diner) struggling to finish his work and having to stay hours into the night just to scrape by. Rather than waiting to be given an assignment or getting angry at a world that treats him and his family this way, the boy sees a need and goes to work trying to fill it.

After weeks of trying, failing, recalculating, and trying again, he is able to invent a working robot that can help his father wash the dishes and tidy the kitchen in no time.

If this young man had instead chosen an employee mind-set, he might have ended up where his father was before too long; if he had chosen a victim mind-set, he would have spent his life hating himself and other people but never doing anything to make his situation better. In

> **If mentors aren't careful, they can shut down entrepreneurship and innovation, which in practice shuts down leadership and success.**

either case, he certainly wouldn't have gone on to make the wonderful inventions or have the big adventures that he later did.

Leaders must be able to see the potential miracle in every downside. Mentors can help them do this by teaching them the power of entrepreneurship and innovation. A good way to help mentees start to think this way is to ask the right questions and even point out opportunities in disguise.

Mentors who constantly discuss and draw attention to hidden opportunities with their mentees will help those mentees build their entrepreneurial mind-sets.

A word of caution: it is important for mentors to recognize and support entrepreneurial endeavors from their mentees. If mentors aren't careful, they can shut down entrepreneurship and innovation, which in practice shuts down leadership and success.

Mentors who throw out their mentees' entrepreneurship are doing them a serious disservice.

Sadly, in *Robots*, the boy's employer does not view his attempt to fill a need lightly and ends up crushing something that could have ultimately made everyone in the situation happier and more successful. Mentors should try to be patient and understanding with early efforts at entrepreneurship from their mentees because those endeavors often lead to huge improvement and greater success for everyone.

As Roger Clemens said, "I think anything is possible if you have the mind-set and the will and desire to do it and put the time in." Mentors and mentees who have the right mind-set, and act on the thoughts and impressions that come with it, will at times accomplish things that previously seemed impossible.

Orrin Woodward said, "While many are saying that it can't be done, leaders are out getting it done." That's what this difference basically boils down to: an employee mind-set excuses those who have it from any action because success is deemed impossible, while the entrepreneurial mind-set leads those who have it to make their success.

Mentors should encourage mentees to avoid the blind-follower mentality of an employee mind-set and adopt a more entrepreneurial worldview. Additionally, mentors should also think entrepreneurially in their own lives and undertakings. Doing so will put focus where it matters and lead to all sorts of seemingly miraculous advancement toward the fulfillment of their dreams.

68

THE MANAGER/
ARTIST BALANCE

Good mentors understand the balancing act between firm instruction and leadership on the one hand and close friendship on the other. They are closer to friendship than dictatorship, but they also know how to take a firm stand. A good mentor learns fairly early that playing the role of drill sergeant in the lives of his mentees is not the most effective way to help them develop leadership or excellence. On the other hand, being too "buddy-buddy" with the protégé is also not good.

Familiarity with the Manager/Artist balance will help mentors lead out and guide their mentees in meaningful ways. The following chart illustrates some of the traits and characteristics of each:[39]

Manager	Artist
Concrete	Abstract
Steady progress	Ups and downs
Avoids crisis	Crisis feeds creativity
Plans	Follows moods
Follows through	Creative
Routine	Eclectic

Good mentors should remember to maintain a proper balance between these two approaches. Doing so will help them create positive and productive relationships with their mentees.

Workshop[40]

First, take the time to go through each of the compared characteristics, and select which one best represents you. For example, ask yourself, "Am I more concrete or abstract?" And continue down the list.

As soon as you've completed the first step, pull out a blank sheet of paper, create the following graph on it, and mark where you think you are.

MANAGER ————————————— ARTIST

Are you closer to Manager or to Artist? Which do you tend to lean toward? Are you right in the center—exactly balanced between Manager and Artist?

Now make a second copy of the chart. Consider where you think you *should* be and mark it on your blank chart.

Doing this will help you set goals and start taking action toward improving your Manager/Artist balance.

To take this exercise a step further, mentors should use this exercise frequently in each of their mentoring relationships. To do this, take out another page, put the chart on it, and write a specific mentee's name on the top.

What is your usual Manager/Artist balance with this specific mentee? What does he need it to be at the moment?

The best Manager/Artist balance is whatever the individual mentee needs right now. Mentors should know this and act accordingly. Sharing this exercise with your mentees will help them significantly improve their own mentoring.

The difference between a friend and a mentor is this: A friend sees your weaknesses and loves you anyway, while a mentor sees your weaknesses and loves you enough to help you change.

69

THE HEALER/ WARRIOR BALANCE

Another important balance for mentors to be aware of is the Healer/Warrior balance. Steven Seagal said, "Any great warrior is also a scholar, and a poet, and an artist." And the very best Warriors are also Healers, like Aragorn in *The Lord of the Rings*. Mentors understand the importance of simultaneously filling many roles in their mentoring, including Manager and Artist, or Warrior and Healer.

The important characteristics to blend when seeking this balance include the following:

Healer	Warrior
Soothes	Provokes
Embraces	Pushes
Comforts	Challenges
Loves	Trains
Relaxes	Leads
Laughs	Analyzes

Understanding and applying this balance will help mentors lead mentees to relationships with the right balance of leadership and love. Mentees need both Healer and Warrior in their mentoring experiences, and the balance naturally changes depending on the mentee and where he or she is on life's path.

The purpose of this balance is to make sure that a leader's mentoring mixes the right amounts of loving and supporting with the necessary portions of pushing and challenging. Mentors should be good friends to their mentees—people they can trust, lean on, and look to for comfort and support. However, mentors do not exist for that purpose alone. Mentors are also supposed to help the mentee find his path and then push and guide him to fight for his success.

> **Mentors are supposed to help the mentee find his path and then push and guide him to fight for his success.**

In order for mentors to be truly effective, they must learn to use the proper balance between the Healer and the Warrior.

Workshop[41]

Repeat the workshop from the last chapter using the characteristics of Healers and Warriors. Begin by asking yourself these questions:

1. Am I more soothing or provoking as a mentor?
2. Are my mentor meetings more like supportive embraces or demanding wind sprints?
3. Do my mentees usually feel loved and relaxed, or trained and challenged?
4. Am I more likely to laugh with my mentees or analyze them?
5. What are my default settings on these qualities? What am I most comfortable with?
6. As a mentor, what is my typical balance of Healer and Warrior?

Make sure you record your answers and thoughts, and keep them so you can look back on them whenever you want. Now, create the following graph on a blank page:

HEALER

WARRIOR

Based on your answers to the previous questions, mark where you think you are on this graph. Then mark where you think you should be. Compare where you think you are with where you think you should be, note the difference, and determine where you need to go from here. Record your findings.

Finally, mark on a new graph where you need to be right now for each of your mentees individually. This last part should shape the way you approach that relationship because leaders should always target their mentoring to the needs of the mentee in question.

Like personality types, learning styles, and love languages, these balances can help you improve how you

231

mentor each mentee, and they can help your protégés work with you more effectively.

70

HAPPINESS IS KEY

Good mentors should be happy! In fact, so should everyone. To be truly successful, people must know that their happiness is entirely in their own hands. The choice to be happy, regardless of circumstances, is one that good mentors should make every day.

Helen Keller said, "Your success and happiness lies in you. Resolve to keep happy, and your joy and you shall form an invincible host against difficulties." The resolution to be happy will not only bring happiness, but it will also make it possible for mentors to find the necessary drive to achieve lasting success.

A classic example of this is found in the book *Pollyanna* by Eleanor H. Porter. The story is about a young orphan girl, Pollyanna, who goes to live with her rich, stern aunt. The thing that sets this girl apart from everyone around her is her attitude about life; she really takes to heart the idea of looking on the bright side. Her philosophy centers on playing the "Glad Game."

The point of the game is to find something to be glad about in every situation. One Christmas, earlier in her life,

Pollyanna found a pair of crutches in a missionary barrel, rather than the doll she was hoping for. The game originated when her father said they could always be glad they didn't need to use them!

Since that Christmas, Pollyanna has gone about life finding the happy situation in every sad one and allowing that to shape her attitude. This allows her to find much more success because no matter what curveballs the world throws at her, *she* is in charge of her happiness, and nobody can take it away from her.

As everyone does, she faces some daunting obstacles, one of which even threatens to make her quit playing the game. But ultimately, she knows that by controlling her happiness, she can control her success, if not her environment and challenges.

> **Mentors who are responsible for their own happiness will be able to *choose* their success in each situation.**

This lesson is absolutely vital to success. Mentors who are responsible for their own happiness will be able to *choose* their success in each situation. Happiness is one of the main parts of success, and mentors who choose their happiness, no matter what, are halfway there. Aside from being a good half of success, happiness will also give mentors the drive and the will to continue with the hard work that will bring them the other half.

As Groucho Marx said, "I, not events, have the power to make me happy or unhappy today. I can choose which it shall be. Yesterday is dead; tomorrow hasn't arrived yet. I have just one day, today, and I'm going to be happy in it."[42]

Mentors and mentees who choose to be happy in each new day will find that their journey to success is filled not only with hard work but also with happiness. As they look for things to be happy about in their lives, they will find that every *little* success matters. This is how great leaders make their lives livable, even fun, and their dreams worth it all.

71

COURAGE

C. S. Lewis said, "Courage is not simply one of the virtues, but the form of every virtue at the testing point."[43] Good mentors know that courage means keeping to their virtues, especially when they're being sorely tested. Virtues, ideals, traits, and principles aren't really worth much if they're not accompanied by the courage that sees them through the tough moments.

Courage is what turns hard work and perseverance into tenacity. It's what turns good manners and nice words into courtesy. And it's what turns the glad game and looking on the bright side into happiness.

It is also what turns tenacity, courtesy, and happiness into actual success. Maya Angelou said, "Courage is the most important of all the virtues, because without courage you can't practice any other virtue consistently. You can practice any virtue erratically, but nothing consistently without courage."

Mentors know that in order to achieve their dreams, they need to have the courage to be their very best selves, even when it would be easier to be some lesser version.

Without courage, there is no real virtue, and without virtue, there is no real success. Because of this, as Anaïs Nin put it, "Life shrinks or expands in proportion to one's courage." Mentors who want real success must be willing to live their virtues, regardless of fear, pain, discomfort, or hardship, and they must teach their mentees to do the same.

> To be strong and influential leaders, mentors need to have the courage to stand for the right things, even when it's difficult.

A person who has big dreams is going to face a lot of big obstacles between himself and those dreams. In fact, overcoming obstacles is one of the things that make a person really successful. Obstacles, tests, hardships, difficulties—these are the natural steps on the path to real happiness and accomplishment. There is no way to avoid them, but there are many ways to overcome them and learn from them. All of those ways take courage.

To be strong and influential leaders, mentors need to have the courage to stand for the right things, even when it's difficult. A protégé can be empowered and helped by his mentor's example of courage and strength. And, as a famous John Wayne quote goes, "Courage is being scared to death...and saddling up anyway." Or as business leader Claude Hamilton says, "Keep your helmet on!"

72

DEFIANCE

Gravity is one of the oldest laws on the books, as well as one of the best known. Even small children generally understand that when Mommy lets go of the pencil she's holding out, the pencil will fall to the ground. This is fact, and everybody knows it.

Good mentors defy gravity.

While the unquestionable nature of the "fact" of gravity would seem to suggest that defying it is impossible, the *fact* remains that people have been conquering gravity for centuries.

As early as 428–347 BC, philosopher and inventor Archytas claimed to have created the first self-propelled flying device. It was even said to have flown in public for at least two hundred meters. This was an unmanned device, but according to witnesses, it did fly. Since then, hundreds of others have claimed to have created a flying machine or even to have flown themselves.

Of course, modern science tells us that these machines, such as hot air balloons, airplanes, and human gliders, were not acting in defiance of gravity—that they in fact *used* gravity to achieve their goals.

> **The law of lift overcomes the law of gravity.**

Yet this completely fits within the definition of defiance. The law of lift overcomes the law of gravity.

The great leaders in science and technology showed us one thing: gravity is not ruler over humanity. Conformity to "the rules" can hold us back and limit us. Understanding that humans have the power to use gravity in ways they hadn't thought of before set these individuals free, and they accomplished mind-boggling and world-shifting things because of it.

Now what does this have to do with being good mentors? It applies in at least two very important ways:

1. Great mentors must learn that success means asking the right questions (instead of blindly believing everything they are told) and working with their environment to make their dreams come true. They don't have to let their environment, or the people they interact with, keep them down. They use that environment and shape the future they want.

Then, with a lot of hard work and faith, they make things happen. Really successful people don't say, "Gravity means people can't fly." Instead they go out and build themselves a hang glider, using the laws of gravity.

That said, great mentors should never let anyone negatively control their environment or bring them down. No one should be able to stop them from achieving their dreams.

2. The young child knows that when his mother drops the pencil, it will fall. But what if she doesn't drop it? A great mentor knows not to drop the pencil until he wants it to fall. He can devise ways to tie it up so he can rest his hand, or he can simply place it in his pocket. The second important way mentors can defy gravity is by remembering this simple rule: a person with ingenuity and initiative can and will find ways to get around obstacles and limitations, if he is willing to think and work hard.

Mentors who really want to make a difference and realize their dreams must learn to say, with the heroine of the Broadway musical *Wicked*, "I'm through accepting limits, 'cause someone says they're so—some things I cannot change, but till I try, I'll never know....It's time I tried defying gravity!"[44]

Mentors who do this and teach their mentees to do the same will reach new heights of achievement and success.

73

WHO DO YOU LISTEN TO?

Mentors must learn for themselves and teach their mentees the power of listening to the right voices. The world is full of all sorts of voices, demands, suggestions, advice, and counsel. Leaders must learn to pick out the *right* voices and listen to them, ignoring all the wrong ones.

A person will not get very far if he tries to listen to every piece of advice he gets from anyone. Between parents, TV commercials, neighbors, magazine ads, children, self-help books, friends, and so on (let's face it, the list is endless), a person would be sent in so many directions at once that he wouldn't even be able to move.

Unfortunately, it's fairly easy to pick the wrong advisers, and people do it all the time. The problem with this is that a person who picks a few wrong advisers will get somewhere and fast. Sadly, the somewhere

> **If a person will learn to shut out all the negative voices and listen only to the few that matter, he or she will learn how to become one of those few who lead.**

he'll be getting is not a very desirable place. People who

choose to listen to the wrong voices may never know what they miss out on, but often it's huge success and happiness.

On the flip side, if a person will learn to shut out all the negative voices and listen only to the few that matter, he or she will learn how to become one of those few who lead. There are a lot of unhelpful voices out there saying what cannot be done, but those who will instead note the ones who are actually doing what it takes to realize their dreams—and listen to those people—will learn how to reach success, instead of believing that there is no way.

Sidney Sheldon said, "Don't give up. There are too many naysayers out there who will try to discourage you. Don't listen to them. The only one who can make you give up is yourself." What he didn't say, but which is nevertheless true, is that while the naysayers can't stop a person without his consent, the yea-sayers can really help lift him up and give him powerful advice.

Mentors should make a point of listening to people who really know what they're talking about. If they want advice on their garden, they should take the words of the gardener over those of the mechanic. However, if they want advice on their vehicle, the mechanic is a better choice than the gardener. If they want medical advice, they should seek out a doctor, not a lawyer.

When a person wants to be a great mentor, he should listen to the advice and counsel of great leaders. When a person wants to be a great leader, she should listen to the words and guidance of great mentors. The person who wants to know success needs to seek and listen to the mentoring of truly successful people and put that mentoring into action.

Just as he shouldn't go to a hairstylist to learn about carpentry, a man should not go to people who have achieved little success to learn about how to succeed.

Great mentors should teach their mentees about the necessity of listening to the people who actually know what they're talking about. There are real ways to achieve success, and listening to the people who have paid the price and earned success is a much better way to get there than listening to people who still don't believe it's possible.

> **Great mentors don't let the advice of the doubters stop them from listening to and following the wisdom of the doers.**

Great mentors don't let the advice of the doubters stop them from listening to and following the wisdom of the doers. And they encourage their mentees to adopt the same philosophy.

The shortest path to success (or through a mine field) is in the footsteps of someone who has safely made it across.

74

SECURITY

Good mentors understand that being busy isn't good for its own sake, and certainly feeling *too* busy actually damages the ability of a person to effectively accomplish the things that matter to her. As Richard Paul Evans put it, "The law of centrifugal force seems to be as true for the human condition as it is for the Newtonian mechanics. The faster our lives spin, the more things tend to fly apart."[45] People who allow themselves to get overwhelmed get less done than those who are able to focus on what matters and, specifically, their next step.

The solution to finding true security and dismissing overwhelming and limiting attitudes is to know that you are doing the right thing and doing it effectively. Mentors who take the time to challenge themselves and come to understand these two things will be able to face huge challenges and obstacles without getting overwhelmed or distracted by them.

Mentors should be prayerful in determining what's right for them so they can achieve the first step to being "Secure, Not Stressed."[46] Knowing that he's doing the right thing will make a world of difference to the security of the mentor, and he should help his mentees attain this level of purpose and awareness so they can enjoy the security that comes with knowing they're on the right path.

The second step can be more difficult to track, but it is just as important. Some mentors prefer to try every alternate possibility of mentoring, for years, until they come up with something they are *sure* works effectively for them. This can bring success, but it is a long process.

Another way to achieve success in this area is to learn from what past mentors have done and how they achieved success. This is the smart way to learn effective mentoring because it utilizes the available tools rather than relying on the abilities of one mentor, spread over a number of years.

Few people achieve a completely stress-free life. But if a person pays the price to know that he's doing the right thing and that he's doing it well, this will significantly reduce stress and at the same time boost his feelings of security and his actual effectiveness.

As mentors learn of, implement, and master this tool, they will find that they are usually more prepared to apply all the other techniques of great mentoring.

Mentors who are secure instead of stressed will be able to accomplish more, feel happier, and influence their mentees to do the same—because while the disease of the twenty-first century is contagious, so is its cure. Mentors should teach their mentees the power of having security in their vision and in their actions. This will free up their focus and make their path clearer and easier to follow.

Knowing that he's going in the right direction will make the mentee happier and more driven to keep moving forward.

75

FIND RENEWAL

For leaders, the burdens are sometimes big, the path is sometimes lonely, and the potential to fail or be attacked is sometimes a constant threat. These pressures can certainly take their toll. If leaders become dissatisfied with their results (not because the results aren't the *right* results, but because it's hard and frustrating to achieve them), they can begin to inadvertently compete with their own happiness. The solution, according to Richard Bayatzis and Annie McKee, is renewal.[47] Good mentors understand that along the journey, everyone needs renewal. Renewal can be valuable and healing after challenges or trials, when a person simply gets worn out, or sometimes just to boost one's interest and commitment.

At times, merely taking a little break is enough to renew and refresh someone's purpose and drive. As Diane Dettmann said, "It is not the time that heals, but what we do within that time that creates positive change."[48] That said, here are six steps for smart mentors to use in order to find refreshing and successful renewal in life.

STEP 1: REALIZE YOU NEED A RENEWAL

R. D. Laing wrote, "The range of what we think and do is limited by what we fail to notice. And because we fail to notice that we fail to notice, there is little we can do to change; until we notice how failing to notice shapes our thoughts and deeds." This is an

> **Renewal can be as simple as playing a game of basketball or as significant as taking a trip to Italy.**

important depiction of why it's so important to realize the need for a renewal. When people don't recognize their needs, they really can't act to fulfill them.

Mentors should become aware of their state of mind and being and then make an honest assessment. Holding back from taking necessary renewal time is not the brave or helpful thing to do. When you need a break to find meaningful renewal, it's okay to take it. Of course you shouldn't live your life as one big party or never-ending vacation. But taking the time to renew yourself, your drive, your vision, and your purpose is vital to your success and happiness.

Renewal can be as simple as playing a game of basketball or as significant as taking a trip to Italy. Some people play golf to renew; others read or walk in the park. Whatever the activity, leaders need times of renewal, times to recharge, regenerate, and refocus. And often, times of renewal are effective times of assessing and changing things.

In fact, bestselling author Chris Brady wrote a great book on the importance of renewal entitled *A Month of Italy*. This book can help leaders understand the impact that appropriate renewal can have on their life success and happiness. When you or the people you work with want to learn more about the importance and power of renewal, read *A Month of Italy*.

STEP 2: TAKE RESPONSIBIITY FOR YOUR OWN RENEWAL

Once they've recognized their need for renewal, good mentors should take responsibility and act. Renewal doesn't happen overnight just because someone notices she needs it. Good mentors understand that they must take responsibility for renewing themselves and for doing it effectively.

Mentors should help mentees understand that they too are responsible for their own renewal. While a good mentor can help her mentees know when they need it and how to do it best, ultimately the mentee has to be in charge of his own renewal.

Mentors should be helpful and encouraging to their mentee's renewal, but they should make it clear that at the end of the day, it's up to *him* to make it happen.

STEP 3: VISUALIZE — WHAT DO YOU WANT? SEE IT, TASTE IT, LIVE IT

Renewal isn't just a time of vacation. It is a time for mentors and mentees to reimmerse themselves in the *why* of what they do. Often people forget what they're working for and just remember how hard they're working. Visualizing their dream and taking time to remember what it's all about can really make a difference in the way they work.

> **Renewal isn't just a time of vacation. It is a time for mentors and mentees to reimmerse themselves in the *why* of what they do.**

STEP 4: SEE THE NEEDS OF THE WORLD AND HOW YOU CAN HELP

Mentors who sometimes take a step back and look at the big picture, and then focus on the little things they can do to improve, generally feel empowered and inspired to start doing the little things more effectively.

STEP 5: OUTLINE YOUR LEARNING PACKAGE

To really optimize renewal time, good mentors understand that they must make a plan to put into use the things they learn and experience during renewal and self-searches. To do this, mentors can ask themselves five important renewal questions before they settle back into the daily grind:

a. *What do I need to know?* Part of renewal is identifying knowledge and skills mentors want to obtain.

b. *What do I need to do?* Mentors should also come out of renewals with a specific idea, or list of ideas, on what they need to do to better achieve their success and realize their dreams.

c. *What do I need to feel?* Often what a person feels is more powerful than what he thinks because it automatically has his passion behind it. Leaders should not walk away from renewals without strong and powerful feelings of renewed resolve, vision, and excitement about their work and life. They should also be aware of other feelings this renewal has given them, and how they can learn from them and use them to increase their effectiveness.

d. *What do I not want?* Coming out of renewal with a clear idea of what he does not want is a fantastic way for a person to throw out any of the old and insignificant hardship from his previous journey and walk forward with both the power of specific intent and the security of meaningful goals and work on his side.

e. *What do I want?* Likewise, knowing what he *does* want will help him to choose the right actions and analyze results for effectiveness or failure so he can redirect and improve his work-to-success ratio.

STEP 6: GET BACK TO WORK!

Excellent leaders know that to make a renewal truly successful, they have to continue their fight afterward with the new strength and direction it's given them.

They implement the things they learned from the other five steps, keep a smile on their faces, and continue on their path.

Mentors who understand the importance of renewal and employ these techniques to optimize their resting times will find that they are more inspired and driven to face and overcome challenges and advance toward their dreams and their success. Renewal is not just rest; it's restoration.

76

THINK LIKE A REVOLUTIONARY

The world is full of people who go with the flow and stick to the system. As Guy Kawasaki teaches,[49] the importance of challenging old thinking, and fighting a revolution against mediocrity and resistance to change, is key in genuine leadership and success.

Here are some guidelines Kawasaki recommends to help mentors and mentees to think like revolutionaries:

1. Look for the opposite of the obvious answer. In many cases, the obvious answer is obvious because everyone uses it. Well, in a world where most people do not choose to become authentic

leaders and excellent mentors, the few who do probably don't want to use the same answers and fixes that are accepted by "most people."

Leaders look for the *best* answer, not the obvious or easy one, and then they follow it. Start by looking for the opposite of the norm, and then look deeper to find the *right* choice.

2. Start at the goal and work backward. While most people are making their plans based on what they have to do now, great revolutionaries decide what they *want* and then work out the step-by-step guide on how they can get it. Start with the big picture, and then reframe into smaller, more manageable chunks.

START WITH THE END IN MIND.

3. Always search for the cause of something unexpected. Events that seem random or arbitrary rarely are. Good mentors should learn to look past the unexpectedness to find the meaning within those events. Doing so can help mentors understand the world in new and improved ways, and it can also help them increase their ammunition against the forces of decline.

This is not the kind of curiosity that killed the cat. Rather, it's the kind that led to the big discoveries and shaped the minds of the most powerful innovators and leaders in history.

4. Leave market research to the amateurs, not the professionals. Kawasaki says that leaving the

most important things like finding out about customers and competition to amateurs actually ensures that it will happen in a more effective way because amateurs think like the general public, while professionals often think in statistics, jargon, and intricacy.

In mentoring, this principle means that mentors have to go about their work like "regular" people, not professionals. It's about simplicity over complexity and personalization over mass labeling. Mentors

> **Mentors should understand and utilize the tools of the professional but not get caught up in the abstract generalizations that are his weakness.**

should understand and utilize the tools of the professional but not get caught up in the abstract generalizations that are his weakness.

5. Don't ask; just watch. By watching instead of asking, mentors learn from what mentees are actually doing, not just what they say. This helps mentors understand the reality of what's going on, as well as what's needed. Asking, however, shows only what would be going on if the mentee met his ideals, or perhaps what the mentee thinks is going on, if he's particularly forthcoming.

251

Good mentors should understand and see what mentees do, not just what they say. This will help them pinpoint the needs of the mentees and plan future challenges and projects.

When mentors declare their independence from the norm of mediocrity, launch a personal revolution of leadership and excellence, and then follow through, they open their minds in new ways and find unforeseen and exciting opportunities to influence people and change the world.

77

SEVEN GREAT MENTORS

Every great mentor and mentee has benefited from the influence of different types of mentors throughout his or her life. Recognizing the different kinds, and learning to optimize the relationship with each one, will help leaders achieve their dreams by helping them listen to the right people in the right ways.

Author Tiffany Earl wrote that there are at least seven types of mentors[50] for everyone on the path to success.

The first type of mentor is the *parent mentor*. This is often an informal mentoring relationship, but it is vastly important. Great mentors know that their children matter, and passing on the principles of leadership, success, and mentoring to their own children is one of the most important parts of being a mentor.

Mentors should be powerful but appropriate mentors to their children—remembering the Manager/Artist balance and the Healer/Warrior balance as they deal with young minds and tender feelings—and they should encourage their mentees to do the same.

> **Parenting is one of the greatest responsibilities of real leaders, and they must be careful not to sacrifice the success of their family for the success of their business.**

Parenting is one of the greatest responsibilities of real leaders, and they must be careful not to sacrifice the success of their family for the success of their business. Ultimately, they will be happier if they take the time and put in the work to make *both* successful.

The second type of mentor is the *friend mentor*. This kind of mentoring relationship is also usually informal. A friend mentor is a friend, family member, or acquaintance with whom a person just seems to connect. These are the mentors people go to for strength and support in times of hardship. This type of mentor has many important lessons to teach. Friend mentors are there to listen, to guide, to admonish occasionally, to carry when needed, and to love always.

Good mentors should recognize the relationships in which they play the role of friend mentor and be careful to set the right kind of example and teach the right kind of lessons.

The third type of mentor is the *expert mentor*. Expert mentors are exactly what the term sounds like—people with expertise in a specific field to whom mentors and mentees look for advice and help in that area. Sometimes a person doesn't know his expert mentor personally, but he learns from the mentor's lectures, books, audios, and other materials.

It is very important for mentors and mentees to look to expert mentors specifically on their paths to success because learning from experts is one of the best ways to avoid unnecessary mistakes, difficulty, and pain.

Many mentors should become expert mentors by making their wisdom and guidance available in ways that can reach more than just their formal mentees. This means writing, public speaking, and other venues that allow for wide reach.

A fourth type of mentor is the *educational mentor*. Educational mentors help their mentees acquire the basic skills and learn the basic steps of leadership and success. These mentors guide their mentees through challenges, trials, and difficulties, and they help them learn the vital leadership lessons that are found in each of those obstacles. Educational mentors are generally found in a formal relationship, meaning there is a specific agreement or understanding between mentor and mentee.

Educational mentors also inspire their mentees to read, learn, and gain the superb education that will prepare them for leadership and impact.

The fifth type of mentor is the *dream mentor*. This is another formalized mentoring relationship, but the focus is to help the mentee achieve her dreams. This mentor shares the same basic vision and dream as his mentee, but he's a few steps ahead on the path and thus can share needed wisdom and guidance with the one who walks behind him.

A sixth type of mentor is the *leadership mentor*. In this relationship, mentees and mentors focus on building important things that improve finances and family and ultimately improve the world. Every good leader has at least one leadership mentor, and often many, whose help has drastically leveraged his or her success.

The seventh type of mentor is the *epiphany*. Great mentors and successful mentees learn to take mentoring not only from people, books, and other sources around them, but also from their own thoughts and impressions. Mentors who are looking for it can find inspiration and guidance from all sorts of experiences and circumstances. The lessons are out there, and mentors should keep their eyes and hearts open to them—and teach their mentees to do the same.

Understanding these levels and types of mentoring, and the importance of each, will help mentors take advantage of them all and be better mentors themselves. Also, as their mentees learn to look for them, they will be more effective as well.

EPILOGUE

We Can All Be Mentors!

The word *mentor* comes from Greek mythology, particularly Homer's *Odyssey*.

Mentor was a good friend of Odysseus, and he was entrusted with the care of Odysseus' entire household (including the raising and teaching of his son, Telemachus) while Odysseus traveled with the coalition against Troy.

Mentor was well known for his honesty and integrity, great friendship, gentleness, and kindness accompanied by a willingness to speak out forcefully when the situation required it.

After Odysseus had been gone for many years, many people believed he had been killed during his journey. Men from his domain began to look on the fairness of his wife, Penelope, and many even became her suitors, attempting to gain her hand in marriage. They became a bothersome lot, particularly to the still-loyal Penelope.

Sadly, the young Telemachus didn't know what to do about the suitors. He didn't know if his father was dead or alive, so he wasn't sure if it was even appropriate for these men to pursue his mother. He was also young and timid, afraid to step in at all even if he felt it was right.

This was a difficult time for the family; they missed their husband, father, and master. Penelope did her best to keep the suitors at bay, and Mentor attempted to get the law to step in, but Telemachus remained unsure and inactive.

Perhaps because of the excellent characteristics displayed by Mentor, or possibly for some secret reason of her own, the goddess Athena chose to impersonate Mentor in order to impart her wisdom and advice to the young and less experienced boy. Interestingly, it was she who became a great mentor and guide to Telemachus in this story, all the time wearing the face and voice of Mentor.

> **By the end of the story, Telemachus became a brave and virtuous man, a man ready to face the challenges of the world and to be victorious and successful.**

She came to Telemachus several times in the form of his adviser and counseled him in wisdom and courage. She advised him to search for his father and directed him all along this path. She guided him gracefully through his encounters with foreign powers, and eventually he was reunited with his father, who came back to challenge and ultimately defeat the suitors—all under the careful watch and guidance of Athena in the shape of Mentor.

By the end of the story, Telemachus became a brave and virtuous man, a man ready to face the challenges of the world and to be victorious and successful.

"Mentor" (Athena in disguise) helped him become the man he wanted to be by giving him ideas and direction, as well as loving support. The guidance of this great person was pivotal in the success of the young man. Indeed, it made all the difference. As she inspired him to work hard and improve himself constantly, he grew more and more toward the goal—true manhood.

Ever since this ancient myth was told, the word *mentor* has been used to describe a wise and trusted adviser or guide, someone who shares personal wisdom and the benefit of experience and knowledge with another person.

One thing that makes this story particularly special is that Mentor set an example of excellence, exemplified the best traits, and sought to help and motivate his (her) mentee to reach his highest potential and success.

Mentor became an archetype that anyone can fill—if he or she is willing to put in the work and become the right kind of person.

Another particularly relevant aspect of the myth is that it portrays the positive of mentors as part of God's work. Our service of others builds God's kingdom. Mentoring is so important that a goddess in the myth came to do it, though she took on the role of a man, because ultimately mentoring is something mere mortals can and should do. In this story, the mentor was played by a heavenly being, but she didn't do anything that an earthly one could not have. She inspired her mentee's character and abilities in order to fulfill a higher purpose.

Finally, Mentor himself was a wise man, but one without any supernatural abilities. He was given stewardship over the raising and teaching of Telemachus, but he did not have any special powers to enable him to do this. Great mentors who fulfill their roles as best they can often find that special gifts and help come to them from above.

Mentoring can be part of God's work, and He will enable the mentor to complete the task.

At one point during the poem, Telemachus expressed his worries to Mentor that he was not clever enough to say things well or strong enough to hold his own in the tasks he had been given. Mentor's response should be a lesson to every mentor, to be applied to themselves and taught to each mentee: "Telemachus, where your native wit fails, heaven will inspire you. It is not for nothing that [heaven has] watched your progress ever since your birth."

Everyone has the potential to be a good mentor. We must work tenaciously to achieve it, maintain our focus, and rely on heaven for help. People who are willing to work and who improve themselves constantly, trusting the process and trusting God, will eventually find success. And through excellent mentoring, they can help many others do the same.

In short, mentoring *matters*. Those who have great mentors know this well. Those who are great mentors take action and help others succeed. This is great service.

> **Great mentors help regular people do extraordinary things.**

In the future, as in the past, many will see men and women do great things and wonder how they contributed so much. Those who understand leadership know the answer: great mentors help regular people do extraordinary things.

Our invitation to you is to be a great mentor. The techniques and tools in this book will help you. Your own mentors have set the example. A world of people out there needs what only your unique, passionate service can deliver.

We need you to be a mentor. You can be a great one. Make a decision to mentor. Record the tips to success in this book—then put them into action.

Nothing in your life will bring you more happiness, success, or leadership opportunities than your dedicated *I know!* service. Look around. See what needs to be done, and do it. Improve the world.

A great secret of leadership is this: If you want to change the world in small ways, take action. If you want to change the world in medium ways, join your actions with those of others. But if you want to change the world in big ways, join with others to take action while you mentor future leaders!

NOTES

1. See Orrin Woodward, *RESOLVED* (Flint, MI: Obstaclés Press, 2011).

2. See Oliver DeMille, *A Thomas Jefferson Education* (Cedar City, UT: George Wythe College Press, 2000).

3. Chris Brady and Orrin Woodward, *Launching a Leadership Revolution* (Flint, MI: Obstaclés Press, 2011).

4. Oliver DeMille and Tiffany Earl, *The Student Whisperer* (TJEdOnline, 2011).

5. Brady and Woodward, *Launching*.

6. For ideas on how to do this, see Oliver DeMille and Rachel DeMille, *Leadership Education* (TJEdOnline, 2010).

7. Ibid.

8. Ibid.

9. DeMille and Earl, *Student Whisperer*.

10. Maynard Webb, *Rebooting Work* (San Francisco: Jossey-Bass, 2013), 144–145.

11. Chris Brady, "AND (The Art of the Both)," http://chrisbrady.typepad.com/my_weblog/2013/04/and-the-art-of-the-both.html.

12. Prasad Kaipa and Navi Radjou, *From Smart to Wise* (San Francisco: Jossey-Bass, 2013).

13. Francis Bacon, "Of Goodness and Goodness of Nature" In *Essays or Counsels, Civil and Moral* (Whitefish, MT: Kessinger, 2010).

14. Caroline Myss, *Archetype Cards* (Carlsbad, CA: Hay House, 2003).

15. William Shakespeare, *Twelfth Night*.

16. Larry Bossidy and Ram Charan, *Execution: The Discipline of Getting Things Done* (New York: Crown Business, 2002).

17. Kenneth Blanchard and Spencer Johnson, *The One-Minute Manager* (New York: William Morrow, 1981).

18. Brady and Woodward, *Launching*.

19. See *The Diary and Sundry Observations of Thomas Edison,* edited by Dagobert D. Runes (New York: Philosophical Library, 2007).

20. See DeMille, *A Thomas Jefferson Education.*

21. Mark Twain, *Pudd'nhead Wilson* (New York: Dover, 1999).

22. Alex Knapp, "Five Leadership Lessons from Christopher Nolan's Batman Trilogy," *Forbes* July 30, 2012.

23. Ralph Waldo Emerson, "The Method of Nature," http://www.emersoncentral.com/methnature.htm.

24. Ralph Waldo Emerson, "Self-Reliance," http://www.emersoncentral.com/selfreliance.htm.

25. John Assaraf, *The Complete Vision Board Kit* (New York: Atria, 2008).

26. Helen Keller, *We Bereaved* (n.p.: Leslie Fulenwider, Inc., 1929).

27. Jackie Robinson, *I Never Had It Made* (New York: HarperCollins, 1995).

28. Stephen Covey, *The 7 Habits of Highly Effective People* (New York: Simon and Schuster, 2004).

29. Bill Barnett, "Five Steps to Assess Your Strengths," *Harvard Business Review,* November 29, 2011.

30. Eleanor Roosevelt, *You Learn By Living* (New York: Harper and Row, 1960).

31. Brady and Woodward, *Launching.*

32. DeMille and Earl, *Student Whisperer.*

33. Ibid. Used by permission.

34. Orrin Woodward and Chris Brady, *LIFE* (Flint, MI: Obstaclés Press, 2011).

35. Daniel Coyle, *The Little Book of Talent: 52 Tips for Improving Your Skills* (New York: Bantam, 2012).

36. Ibid.

37. Jodi Picoult, *My Sister's Keeper* (New York: Washington Square Press, 2004).

38. Peter Drucker, *Innovation and Entrepreneurship: Practice and Principles* (New York: HarperCollins, 2009).

39. DeMille and Earl, *Student Whisperer*, used by permission.

40. Ibid.

41. Ibid.

42. Groucho Marx, *The Essential Groucho: Writings by, for and about Groucho Marx*, edited by Stefan Kanfer (New York: Penguin, 2004).

43. C. S. Lewis, *The Screwtape Letters* (New York: HarperCollins, 2001).

44. Stephen Schwartz, "Defying Gravity" from *Wicked.*

45. Richard Paul Evans, *Lost December* (New York: Simon and Schuster, 2011).

46. DeMille and DeMille, *Leadership Education.*

47. Richard Boyatzis and Annie McKee, *Resonant Leadership* (Boston: Harvard Business School, 2005).

48. Diane Dettmann, *Twenty-Eight Snow Angels: A Widow's Story of Love, Loss and Renewal* (Parker, CO: Outskirts Press, 2011).

49. Guy Kawasaki, *Rules for Revolutionaries* (New York: HarperCollins, 2000).

50. DeMille and Earl, *Student Whisperer.*

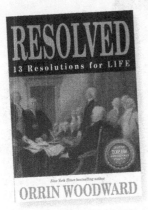

LLR SERIES

Everyone will be called upon to lead at some point in life—and often at many points. The question is whether people will be ready when they are called. The LLR Series is based upon the *New York Times* bestseller *Launching a Leadership Revolution*, in which the authors Chris Brady and Orrin Woodward teach about leadership in a way that applies to everyone. Whether you are seeking corporate or business advancement, community influence, church impact, or better stewardship and effectiveness in your home, the principles and specifics taught in the LLR Series will equip you with what you need.

Subscribers receive 4 CDs and 1 leadership book each month. Topics covered include finances, leadership, public speaking, attitude, goal setting, mentoring, game planning, accountability and progress tracking, levels of motivation, levels of influence, and leaving a personal legacy.

Subscribe to the LLR Series and begin applying these life-transforming truths to your life today!

The LLR (Launching a Leadership Revolution) Series – dedicated to helping people grow in their leadership ability.
4 CDs and 1 book are shipped each month.
$50.00 plus S&H
Pricing is valid for both USD and CAD.

Don't Miss Out on the 3 for FREE Program!

When a Customer or Member subscribes to any one or more packages, that person is given the further incentive to attract other subscribers as well. Once a subscriber signs up three or more Customers on equivalent or greater dollar value subscriptions, that person will receive his or her next month's subscription FREE!

AGO SERIES

Whether you have walked with Christ your entire life or have just begun the journey, we welcome you to experience the love, joy, understanding, and purpose that only Christ can offer. This series is designed to touch and nourish the hearts of all faith levels as our top speakers and special guests help you enhance your understanding of God's plan for your life, marriage, children, and character, while providing valuable support and guidance that all Christians will find beneficial. Nurture your soul, strengthen your faith, and find answers on the go or quietly at home with the AGO Series.

The AGO (All Grace Outreach) Series – dedicated to helping people grow spiritually. 1 CD and 1 book are shipped each month. $25.00 plus S&H
Pricing is valid for both USD and CAD.

EDGE SERIES

Designed especially for those on the younger side of life, this is a hard-core, no-frills approach to learning the things that make for a successful life.

Eliminate the noise around you about who you are and who you should become. Instead, figure it out for yourself in a mighty way with life-changing information from people who would do just about anything to have learned these truths much, much sooner in life! It may have taken them a lifetime to discover this wisdom and knowledge, but now you have the opportunity to learn from their experience on a monthly basis.

Edge Series – dedicated to helping young people grow. 1 CD is shipped each month. $10.00 plus S&H
Pricing is valid for both USD and CAD.

FREEDOM SERIES

If you are a freedom-loving citizen who wants to gain an even greater understanding of the significance and power of freedom, stay informed about the issues that affect your freedom, and find out more about what you can do to reverse any decline and lead the world toward greater liberty, the LIFE Freedom Series is just what you need.

Freedom Series – Dedicated
to helping people understand
the meaning of Freedom.
1 CD is shipped each month.
$10.00 plus S&H
Pricing is valid for both USD and CAD.

RASCAL RADIO

Rascal Radio Subscription – $49.95 per month
Rascal Radio by LIFE Leadership is the world's first online personal development radio hot spot. Rascal Radio is centered on LIFE's 8 Fs: Faith, Family, Finances, Fitness, Following, Freedom, Friends, and Fun. Subscribers have unlimited access to **hundreds and hundreds** of audio recordings that they can stream endlessly from both the LIFE Leadership website and the **LIFE Leadership Smartphone App.** Listen to one of the preset stations or customize your own based on speaker or subject. Of course, you can easily skip tracks or "like" as many as you want. And if you are listening from the website, you can purchase any one of these incredible audios.

Let Rascal Radio provide you with **life-changing information to help you live the life you've always wanted!**

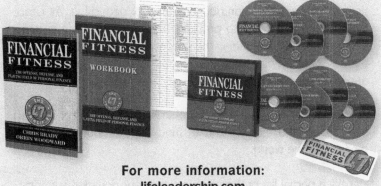

ALL GRACE OUTREACH

All Grace Outreach originally began in 1993 in Maine as "Christian Mission Services." In March of 2007, the organization was transferred to Michigan, and the name was changed to All Grace Outreach. All Grace Outreach is a 501(c)3 charitable organization, which means all contributions are tax deductible. All Grace Outreach is committed to providing assistance to those in need. Our main focus is spreading the gospel of Jesus Christ throughout the world and helping abused, abandoned, and distressed children and widows.

Mission and Vision: To impact and improve the lives of children both locally and globally and to fund Christian outreach efforts throughout the world.

Here is a partial list of the organizations your donation supports:

Founders Ministries
A New Beginning Pregnancy Center
PLNTD
GAP Ministries
Wisdom for the Heart
Samaritan's Purse
Milwaukee Rescue Mission
Ligonier Ministries
Shepherds Theological Seminary
Zoie Sky Foundation

www.allgraceoutreach.com